NEGOTIATION

Praise for *Negotiation: How to Craft Agreements that Give Everyone More*

'In today's business world, many people forget the simple message of this book: that collaboration is a useful and successful strategy for success. I particularly like the practical advice and step-by-step guides to applying this strategy in all areas of your life where you need to seek agreement. If there is one book about negotiation I can thoroughly recommend you have on your shelf, it's this one.'

Kathleen Saxton, Founder and CEO, The Lighthouse Company

'Gavin's is a special gift. If you have spent time with him, you will want to spend time with this book. If this is your first exposure to his talent, you are in for a treat.'

Marc Nohr, CEO, Fold7, former *FT* Columnist and Founder of Kitcatt Nohr

'It's great to read such an honest, practical and enjoyable guide to the art of negotiation. I've been using this type of material with my own clients for many years, so I know how helpful it will be for anyone who needs to negotiate to get results. It's definitely something I would recommend to any salesperson, buyer or manager in any field.'

Mike Morton, Leadership and Influence Trainer

'Gavin's book is transformational because it provides the solid steps needed for effective negotiation in a simple format that allows people to use it. I've been sharing the practical stories, tools and techniques with my coachees and training participants, and can see how effective this approach is in real life.'

Steven Fine, Master Practitioner, Lumina Learning

'In every area of our business, negotiation skills play a vital role. It's great to see a book that shares our culture of long-term cooperation, and also gives the reader practical skills they can apply to create better agreements. I will recommend that everyone in my team reads this book; if you want your teams to be more successful, I suggest you recommend that they read it too.'

Naren Patel, CEO, Primesight

Gavin Presman

NEGOTIATION

HOW TO CRAFT AGREEMENTS THAT GIVE EVERYONE MORE...

ICON

Published in the UK in 2016 by
Icon Books Ltd, Omnibus Business Centre,
39–41 North Road, London N7 9DP
email: info@iconbooks.com
www.iconbooks.com

Sold in the UK, Europe and Asia
by Faber & Faber Ltd, Bloomsbury House,
74–77 Great Russell Street,
London WC1B 3DA or their agents

Distributed in the UK, Europe and Asia
by Grantham Book Services,
Trent Road, Grantham NG31 7XQ

Distributed in Australia and New Zealand
by Allen & Unwin Pty Ltd,
PO Box 8500, 83 Alexander Street,
Crows Nest, NSW 2065

Distributed in South Africa by
Jonathan Ball, Office B4, The District,
41 Sir Lowry Road, Woodstock 7925

Distributed in India by Penguin Books India,
7th Floor, Infinity Tower – C, DLF Cyber City,
Gurgaon 122002, Haryana

Distributed in Canada by Publishers Group Canada,
76 Stafford Street, Unit 300,
Toronto, Ontario M6J 2S1

Distributed in the USA
by Publishers Group West,
1700 Fourth St., Berkeley, CA, 94710

ISBN: 978-184831-937-0

Text copyright © 2016 Gavin Presman

Typeset in Adobe Caslon by Marie Doherty

Printed and bound in the UK by Clays Ltd, St Ives plc

About the Author

Gavin runs a personal and professional training venture, Inspire, which he launched in 2002. His clients range from leading media and technology businesses, including Microsoft, Guardian Media Group and Twitter, to creative businesses, including Global Radio, Bauer, the How To Academy and We Are Social. He regularly delivers negotiation and influence training across the world, through Inspire, Lumina Learning and DOOR International. A graduate of the One Thought Professional Institute, he runs coaching and training in the business world with Inspiring Insight, and works with pupils and teachers to bring resilience and insight into schools through the Innate Health Centre. He is also the chair of governors at Eden Primary, a new free school he helped found, and a mentor at The House of St Barnabas Employment Academy.

Gavin is the son of a teacher/politician/preacher (and stand-in rabbi) and a City lawyer. Evenings in the Presman household involved little TV and much debate, and Gavin learned from his father the importance of understanding all sides of an argument, from his mother how to use a good story, and from his grandfather how to make a good deal. His Booba didn't teach him much in the field of negotiation, but made a sensational chicken soup.

This book is dedicated to my best friend, my amazing wife Jools, who with her support made it possible.

Angel, without you I am nothing, and to me you are everything.

Contents

Foreword by Bruce Daisley, VP Europe, Twitter   xi

Introduction – Why Good Negotiation
Practice Leads to Better Personal and
Professional Relationships   1

1. Giving Structure to Your Negotiation
    Strategy   11
2. Step One – Preparing Yourself for
    Collaborative Negotiation   23
3. Step Two – Preparing a Plan   39
4. Step Three – Understanding Your Partner's
    Point of View   57
5. Step Four – Discussing   69
6. Step Five – Proposing   97
7. Step Six – Bargaining   107
8. Step Seven – Agreeing   123
9. Understanding the Human Operating
    System   131
10. Understanding Personality Traits for
    Better Negotiations   145
11. Using the Seven Steps at Home   169
12. Avoiding Common Gambits Some
    Negotiators Use   185

Conclusion – Can You Really Get More
by Giving More?   195

Recommended Reading   201
Index   203

Foreword

by Bruce Daisley, VP Europe, Twitter

If you've never faced a tricky negotiation in your life, then you're in a very small – and very lucky – minority. Strangely, for something so everyday, most of us feel daunted and unprepared for these encounters. The prospect of a negotiation can be one of the most anxious anticipations in our lives – we dread the very idea. It seems to represent only the opportunity to lose out. Additionally, we read *negotiation* as *confrontation*. And the 'fight or flight' part of our brain wants to scarper for the hills.

Our lives are brim-full of stories of negotiation. A friend of mine told me how he was ostracized on his week-long dream holiday in the Caribbean when fellow holiday-makers heard he had 'got it cheap'. This is the visceral fear of bargaining situations – we dread them even when they don't involve us. Many of us harbour a fear that our inexpert talents mean that others are getting more out of deals than we are. All of this makes negotiating feel such high stakes.

The remarkable thing about something that can provoke such sleepless nights, is that learning to negotiate better is one of simplest skills that we can begin to master. And literally one of the most rewarding. It's why I was delighted when Gavin Presman – one of my career mentors – decided to write this book. Negotiation is an art that has been honed over centuries. An art that merges an understanding of everything from the human psyche to game theory. But it's also something that can quickly demonstrate our lack of experience. Gavin's approach is concise, clear and easy to use – and it's no surprise that he was asked to commit it to print.

In his use of simple, real-life examples, Gavin stands on the shoulders of giants – bringing in the expertise of some of the zestiest intellects, while making their work easy to understand. The truth about negotiation is that there are no new secret formulas needed. We just need to pay homage to the minds who went before us. Gavin has harvested their labours and imparts them in a way that's easy to use.

Having been trained by Gavin and having learned from him in the past, this book has been a brilliantly stimulating reminder of how a handful of simple techniques can transform what we achieve when properly prepared. Gavin has created the go-to book for everyone.

Why Good Negotiation Practice Leads to Better Personal and Professional Relationships

When I started out in business, if I lost, or lost out, in a negotiation, whatever the context and no matter how much I attempted to post-rationalize, it always felt personal. I had usually expended considerable emotional energy to get myself through it, and the ramifications often continued to haunt me long after I had picked myself up and brushed myself off.

The outcomes of our negotiations, both at work and in our personal lives, have wide-ranging implications. Missed opportunities to negotiate or mismanaged negotiations mean we, and often others, lose out. We can lose out financially, we can lose confidence, and we can lose the respect of others. Sometimes this is because we do not even spot an opportunity to negotiate; sometimes our lack of technique makes us uncomfortable, embarrassed and intimidated, and we rush the negotiation process to get it over with. Among my course attendees, even senior and highly experienced businessmen and businesswomen say they often find negotiation stressful and outcomes dissatisfying.

My own turning point in improving my negotiation skills occurred when someone got the better of me, I took it hard, and it became apparent that I had been played by an expert. I determined to learn from the experience and to take every possible step to avoid repeating my mistakes. This lesson didn't happen in a boardroom, or a customer's office, but in my mother's kitchen, and I wasn't learning from my elders, but rather from Millie, my six-year-old niece. Millie was my bridge to adulthood. I cried when she was born, in the realisation that I had crossed a generational line, but despite our age gap we shared a lot of fun and I soon learned that she was pretty sharp, even at the tender age of six.

I was looking after her at my Mum's for the first time. Keen and eager to please, I had the whole afternoon to play the perfect uncle – best friend, sage and teacher. By 5pm I had done everything Millie wanted all afternoon: I had ridden with her on the two-man reclining bicycles in the park, for another half-an-hour after the point when my legs wanted to go home and rest. I had bought her ice cream and crisps, and I had pieced together puzzles. I was exhausted, but the pleasure of having accomplished my mission far outweighed my fatigue, and I buoyantly gathered Millie's belongings ready to escort her home.

'Come on, Millie. It's time to see Mummy now, so let's put your shoes on –'

'No,' she said, with a single turn of the head.

'Ha, ha. Come on now. Let's put these nice red shoes on. We'd better get going or –'

'No shoes.'

'But –'

'Too tight,' she said, without any explanation as to why they hadn't been too tight an hour before.

I tried waiting for a few minutes … then pleading. Then I tried appealing to her good nature, reminding her of my previous favours, but, as with so many clients I've encountered, previous favours hold no currency once eclipsed by a new and greater need.

I tried getting tough, but Millie wasn't taking any bullying from her best uncle, and she knew how to play me. Seeing her bottom lip quiver I switched mode.

'Look, let's try to figure out a way to get home happy,' I said, putting the shoes down on the middle of the table between us. 'Okay then, so … what shall we do?'

I was employing a technique imparted to me by one of my mentors, John Tulley, a man of humility and understanding who taught me much about how to work with difficult people in difficult times. John always said the magic of asking the other party what to do lay in the handing over of the power, thereby creating a space for cooperation. I had used this to great effect at work. Whether it would be as effective on a six-year-old remained to be seen, but at this point I was prepared to try everything to avert Millie's tears.

I looked at the shoes and waited for Millie to respond. She looked at the shoes, satisfied she was getting her way. Then her eyes scanned the room before fixing on something behind me. She held her stare and grinned, and when I turned around to follow her stare I saw a glass jar filled with homemade chocolate-chip cookies, baked by my mother, probably for the specific purpose of bribing her grandchildren on their regular visits. I kicked myself for not having thought of this earlier.

'Oh, I see. So, if I give you one of Savta's cookies, you will put your shoes on?'

This was a basic rule of negotiation, which I used in business all the time. Find something the other party wants that you can give them at low cost to you, to conclude your deal. I was so relieved that Millie was agreeing to comply I forgot to employ another key rule.

I gave Millie the cookie, and when she had finished it, I smiled.

'Right! Let's get your shoes on.'
'No,' she said with a shake of her head.
'Hey, what about our deal?!'

Millie just leaned back in her chair and counted out two fingers.

'Two shoes, two cookies,' I said, tutting to myself as I remembered an essential rule of negotiation: 'get first, then give'. Always.

To this day I don't know whether Millie had this planned out or just took advantage of my weak position when she realized she was in control of the game. To her that's what it was – a game she immediately recognized, but which I had been slow to recognize, even though I played it every day at work.

At this point I knew it was time to invoke the 'phrase that pays' and frame the agreement conditionally and contextually, requiring Millie to make the first move.

'OK, Millie, if you put your shoes on, then I will give you another cookie.'

Simply framing the agreement with 'If you ..., then I ...' is a world apart from framing it with 'I will ..., if you ...', a difference I will explain in detail in Chapter 8 on bargaining.

So, Millie put her shoes on and got her extra cookie, and we enjoyed a quiet walk back to my sister's – at least until Millie was sick all over her shoes.

From that day, I have put the key principles of negotiating to full use at every opportunity in all areas of my life, and now I teach others to do the same. Rather than panicking or taking things personally, I now find negotiating comes naturally to me and feels as much fun as it no doubt felt to Millie the day she got one over on me. I hope that by using the principles in this book you will enjoy it too.

In the following chapters I will explain the negotiation system that I teach on my courses at Inspire and the How To Academy. It is a system that can be used by anyone in any area of life, professional or personal, to make the experience of negotiating stress-free, amicable and rewarding. I developed it by taking the lessons I have learned over 25 years of personal and professional research into negotiating and business psychology, and by adapting them for today's collaborative business culture. The principles are illustrated using examples and are accompanied by check-lists that enable you to start using these strategies straightaway. Whether you are a property broker or pet walker, you sell for a living or buy, or you want to influence your boss, your best friend or your customers, this book will help you to prepare for and engage in every negotiation and agreement. It will help you to make negotiating a more fulfilling and valuable experience for you.

My late English teacher, Mr Stewart, used to say: 'When you think about others first, you serve yourself best.'Take this into account when you negotiate, because people sense selfishness in others very quickly, and it creates mistrust. When we cooperate we create trust and partnerships that can bear fruit well beyond the narrow issues of the day.

So, this is a book that is based on an ethical approach to negotiation: one that favours cooperation over competition, and which is designed to help you craft agreements that give *everyone* more. If you are looking for tools or techniques that will help you coerce others into agreements designed solely to satisfy your own needs, then this isn't the right place for you. My experience has shown me that the most effective negotiators don't just use 'give and take' as a strategy to get more for themselves, they understand it as the fundamental principle behind effective negotiations. They obsess, therefore, not about what they can get for themselves, but about what they can craft together that will make the whole greater than the sum of its parts. What this means is that they believe that doing a deal and using the resources of both parties creatively will benefit both parties more than not doing a deal. While this approach demands more preparation, more time, and sometimes more effort, it yields more results in the short and the long term.

This book can be read cover to cover as you move from basic to more advanced sections. Or you may want to dip straight into the more advanced sections to find help with a specific challenge, person or outcome. You may want to do both, read it through, and then return occasionally, when specific negotiations call for you to apply these lessons in a critical way.

The most important thing is that you start figuring out how to apply these principles and practising the negotiation techniques. To assist you, each chapter contains a range of practical exercises, examples and summaries. If you follow #CollaborativeNegotiation on Twitter, you will be able to share your experiences and learn from others who are trying out these ideas in the field.

While I wrote this book alone, the ideas in this book did not occur to me without a little help from others. I have been inspired by many experts in this field, from Zig Ziglar to Stephen Covey to Alan Pease. Over the years I have been privileged to be personally trained by some of the world's greatest – Werner Erhard, Richard Bandler, Paul McKenna and Sandra Proctor, to name a few. I have shared training platforms and worked alongside some of the UK's finest trainers, including Mike Morton, Paul Kenny, Stewart Desson and Steven Fine, and have recently been privileged to work for and with both Steven Smith, co-author of *Catalyst* and *Egonomics* and the Partners In Leadership Team, whose exceptional work on accountability makes such a difference to the organizations they serve. The ideas they have shared with me have helped form my thinking and, so, without them this book would not have been possible.

Yet some of my biggest lessons have come from those I have chosen not to name: those I never want to meet again, those I walked away from and those who lost the opportunity of working with me, and with others, because of their determination to focus solely on themselves. I have also omitted the names of certain estate agents (you know who you are). I thank them for showing me what not to do.

CHAPTER 1

Giving Structure to Your Negotiation Strategy

When approaching a negotiation, the truth is that most of us jump into bargaining far too quickly. There's little chance for relationship building, neither party gets the best deal it could have got, and both parties are likely to walk away unsatisfied.

This is why structure is so important in negotiation: learning to plan a negotiation and take it step by step means that you don't rush in and miss opportunities. Understanding where we are in the structure helps us to navigate more effectively to ensure we feel confident that both parties are in the right place to get what they want and what they need from every deal.

Time plays an important role in how you structure your negotiation; you need to take your own and others' timeframes and deadlines into account, as well as recognizing any differences between realistic and desired timeframes. For example, if you are negotiating about a house purchase, you will want to make a deal before someone else does; if you are negotiating another kind of sale, both you and the other party may want key exchanges (the money or the product) in a specified time. Having a structure will help you to navigate through these time-frames without getting lost, and without your partner becoming frustrated or disappointed.

In this book, you'll work through the system I have taught for over twenty years. It's structured around seven key steps and is used by negotiation experts in all walks of life from property and retail to politics and peacemaking. The key change from the classic structure expounded by Gavin Kennedy in his 1997 book, *Kennedy on Negotiation*, is that here you see seven steps, whereas Kennedy proposed eight steps that he summarized into four. At two companies I work with, Inspire and DOOR International, we use a seven-step process which separates your preparation into three distinct stages, allowing you the opportunity to prepare effectively before moving on to four deal-making stages. This extra time spent on preparation always yields dividends in the long term.

The seven steps to effective, collaborative negotiation are:

1. PREPARE YOURSELF MENTALLY
2. PREPARE A PLAN
3. PREPARE TO COLLABORATE
4. DISCUSS
5. PROPOSE
6. BARGAIN
7. AGREE.

In this chapter, we cover the importance of following a process, and introduce how to use the seven-step process. Chapters 2–8 will take each step in turn, showing you how to apply the steps practically in your negotiations. The later chapters then go into greater depth about negotiating with *people* – understanding your own and others' personalities, negotiating at home and in your personal life, and dealing with tricky negotiators.

The first step is to prepare mentally: thinking through what outcome you want from the deal and how you can collaborate with the other party to achieve it. Second, you can begin to prepare a list of what you may be able to offer in any bargaining scenario. Third, you step into your partner's shoes and prepare from *their* perspective. These three steps together ensure that you enter any discussion well prepared. Following this, you sit down to have a discussion with the other party (step four), giving you sufficient information to prepare a proposal (step five) that will enable you to bargain (step six) and finally to agree a mutually beneficial outcome (step seven).

Using this structure will support you to craft agreements that work for both parties, will keep you focused on mutual gain, and will prevent you from pushing for, or accepting, agreements that work for only one party or the other. This book is all about crafting agreements that work better for all parties, but why? It's worth considering why it's so important to structure your agreements to achieve this mutual benefit.

THINK ABOUT IT

Let's take a classic hostage scenario. Imagine a few of your colleagues have been taken hostage in your office building. As yet the scene is unclear, but all we know is that your boss and a few of the senior leaders are being held in the canteen. What's the first thing you do? How can you move forward and keep control of the negotiation to achieve a successful outcome for all? I have asked this question hundreds of times in training rooms across the globe and the results demonstrate interesting tendencies we have as negotiators.

How did you answer the question? Did you try to open a line of dialogue with the hostage takers? Did you look at what you might offer to try to end the standoff? When I've asked this question before, many reply that they would try to open a line of communication to establish what the hostage takers' needs are and start building a dialogue. While it seems like the right answer, it's not what the professionals do in real life. Discussion in any negotiation should come *after* careful preparation. Jumping into discussion without thinking through all the variables can lead to challenging outcomes – particularly in our hostage situation. Without understanding all the variables and exploring both sides' needs, and the needs of the other parties in any agreement, you enter the negotiation less likely to skilfully craft an agreement that works for all.

Before you bargain with anyone, carefully analyse the situation you have in front of yourself. Understand your own position clearly, and imagine the other parties' position too. Also, spend time discussing your assumptions with the other parties, so you can work in partnership to create an agreement that works for all.

DO YOU REALLY WANT TO NEGOTIATE?

One interesting thing about the hostage scenario is that it poses a fundamental question of whether or not you *should* negotiate at all. Many of our governments declare that they will not negotiate with terrorists, and it's an understandable position. Negotiation suggests partnering to achieve common goals, but it might not always be possible to find common goals or identify what a win–win outcome would look like.

WIN–WIN

In our daily lives, we sometimes face dealing with people with whom we really don't want to partner. If you are negotiating with someone you really don't trust or care for, you are going to have a problem getting to win–win. It may not be possible to negotiate. Remember that this book is about how we achieve better relationships with suppliers and partners, as much as it is about the practical tools we use to make deals. Later in the book, we'll look at examples of deals that didn't come through and will discuss knowing when to walk away instead of negotiating a bad outcome.

There is a body of academic research that points to the importance of preparation, both mental and physical, in achieving desired outcomes. Teams of behavioural scientists have been conducting negotiation scenarios with test subjects, testing the impact that preparation has on outcomes. The *Negotiation Journal* and the Harvard Negotiation Research Project (HNRP) cite numerous studies that all suggest the same thing: the more options you have, and the more prepared you are, the better the result is likely to be. The methodology recommended in this book is further supported by research in the *Journal of Economic Psychology* that points towards a clear link between preparation, mental conditioning and results.

Bruce Patton, Roger Fisher and William Ury have conducted research over many years into both the structure and practice of effective negotiations. This work forms the basis of one of the classic negotiation books, *Getting to Yes*. It's worth looking a little at what their research demonstrates. The first thing we can take away is the evidence that negotiators who prepare by writing out clear objectives, and those who commit their thinking to paper, rather than simply having objectives in mind, generally fare better in most negotiation scenarios. Further to this, there seems to be evidence that the more detailed the preparation, the better the results. Why this is the case is not always clear, but my experience suggests that time spent in the planning stage always yields results in increased understanding later on in the negotiation.

DISTINGUISHING NEGOTIATION FROM HAGGLING

When the subject of what I do for a living comes up, new friends are keen to tell me about their latest exploits haggling in the market. This is because it is a common misconception that haggling and negotiation are the same thing – although they very clearly are not. While I love the opportunity to haggle and bargain if the common business culture accepts it, they are miles away from the negotiation strategy and practice we are discussing in this book. It's important to define the difference, so we can be clear when we can and can't genuinely negotiate.

Haggling is the act of reducing the price of an item for sale by various means, usually using tactics involving offering different prices and/or threatening to walk away. I can remember my shock as an eight-year-old in the Old City in Jerusalem when, having agreed to pay my whole summer allowance for a backgammon board, my sister stepped in, berating the trader for taking advantage of me, and proceeded to reduce the price by almost half. I couldn't understand what was going on. I got the same board, but paid a whole lot less. It left me a little confused and very wary of market traders for some time. That is the key challenge with haggling. It's OK if you don't need to trade again, but the exchange is based on a fundamental mistrust, which therefore produces more mistrust and less collaboration.

I once witnessed a very poor attempt at negotiation during a 'dual call' I did with a salesman I was coaching. The salesman (who was selling an annual subscription service) was trying to close a deal and was asked for a discount by his client. In fact, he was asked about how much discount he could give. Instead of negotiating, he started haggling and, even worse, he started doing it in percentages, which ended with the customer paying 10 per cent less than he had offered originally. Afterwards I asked the salesman why he had reduced the price, and he told me it was because he was able to give that level of discount, so he did it in order to build trust and rapport with the client. Interesting. How much trust do you think is built when you tell someone your original price was inflated? That you weren't really telling the truth when you told them the original price?

Negotiation is distinct from haggling because in negotiation we are discussing the full terms and conditions of a deal, not just the price. When we negotiate, we are crafting an agreement, not just arguing about the financials. It's a critical distinction. If the subscription salesman had genuinely negotiated with his customer, he would have started a process where he used variables from either side to add value to the deal. Through discussion and understanding he may have found a way to offer something other than price that was more valuable to the customer. Or he may have found something about the customer that would have warranted providing a discount. This way he could have provided a discount *in exchange* for something of value, leaving the perceived value of his product intact, along with the level of trust.

THINK ABOUT IT

Have you ever left a situation where you have 'haggled' and wondered if you could have got a better deal? Have you ever seen trust reduce as the act of haggling takes place? Whether you enjoy the process or not, have you ever been left wondering whether the object you ended up with was really worth what you paid for it?

---

case study KATHLEEN'S PREPARATION FOR A JOB NEGOTIATION

Let's apply what you've learned in Chapter 1 to some examples to help you see how to put the practical steps into action in real scenarios. While these examples may not directly relate to you, as you see how the principles and tools apply to their situations it will help you develop the skills needed to apply these principles and tools to your personal and professional negotiation challenges. We will work through a few case studies throughout the book, so you can see how to use the tools at each step in the process.

Kathleen is an ambitious Sales Director who works for one of Europe's leading media tech businesses, leading a large team of salespeople and account managers who deliver revenue through a network of agency, client and media contacts. She is driven and very smart. She is also a very capable people manager and a great net-worker, which makes her good at her job. She has returned recently from an extended maternity leave, after having her second child.

She reports to a Commercial Director (CD) who, shortly after her return to work, announces his resignation. Although the busi-ness has launched a search for his replacement through headhunt-ers, Kathleen has a good opportunity to step into his role, and the CEO has initiated a conversation with Kathleen and involved the HR Director. The search has been going on for two months, and she knows there is one good candidate in the frame, whom she knows personally. Kathleen is well informed and able to access good advice through her friend Tim, a former headhunter in the field.

How can Kathleen use the three preparation steps to get herself ready to have a productive conversation with the HR Director about taking on the CD role?

From the checklist on page 22, we know that the first step is to check if she feels she is ready to negotiate for the role: 'Are you equal parties who are ready to negotiate?' She needs to think about herself and her family, and ask herself whether the added commitment is something she wants. The answer being 'yes', she then needs to find out whether the CEO is ready to support her in the role – are they equal parties? She has had several discussions early in the process, but hasn't been formally interviewed, and the CEO has been cagey about offering commitment to giving her the role. Now he has communicated through the HR Director that he wants to 'see if we can move things forward', but being based in the US much of the time, she hasn't seen him face-to-face to discuss. She decides to rearrange her schedule to attend a conference in Barcelona where the CEO is hosting a client panel to speak to him directly. A conversation in a tapas bar, plus the critical one she has with her husband the night before, sets her up to enter the negotiation with confidence on an equal footing, even though she still knows that the company has another option they are considering. While that's not ideal, we seldom start a negotiation in a perfect situation, but 'forewarned is forearmed'.

Now Kathleen knows that she wants to make an agreement (question 2 in the checklist), that she's ready to negotiate as an equal party (question 1), and she has a sense that the CEO wants to make an agreement with her (question 3).

Kathleen knows the business well, so feels strongly that she can create long-term value for the company by taking on the position (question 4 in the checklist).

Finally, she needs to make sure that she is mentally prepared to structure the negotiation in such a way that it will produce a collaborative outcome (question 5). Her relationship with an expert in the field, the ex-headhunter Tim, puts her in a good position, as do her conversations with the CEO and HR manager, her husband and the outgoing CD. We will come back to Kathleen's scenario in Chapter 3 to see how she applied this preparation to craft an agreement that worked for her and the business.

For your own negotiations, it's enough at this stage to ask the checklist questions; you don't need to answer all of them, but they will guide you to decide whether you are ready to negotiate. If not, they will help you to figure out what you need to do to put yourself in a better position to create a genuinely collaborative agreement.

CHECKLIST FOR BEFORE YOU NEGOTIATE

There are a few things to consider before you enter your negotiation preparation.

1. Are you equal parties who are ready to negotiate?

2. Do you want to make an agreement with the other party?

3. Do they want to make an agreement with you?

4. Are you expecting to create long-term value for the other person from this agreement or subsequent agreements?

5. Are you mentally prepared to structure the negotiation in such a way that it will produce a collaborative outcome?

If you can't answer 'yes' to the questions in the checklist, then it's worth working on those issues *before* you try to negotiate an agreement. If you are trying to negotiate a deal with someone you don't want to work with in the long term, or if you are not interested in long-term value, don't waste your time reading further. Give this book to someone who works in a business that needs its customers to come back time and time again to create real value, or someone who wants their relationships to last beyond the value of what they can give or get in the moment.

CHAPTER 2

Step One – Preparing Yourself for Collaborative Negotiation

There is a difference in the way this book is written compared to most books on negotiation. It's probably why you picked up this one, and not the many others that would teach you win–win as a strategy to get more of what you want. The critical difference is believing in win–win not just for yourself, but because you want your partner to get more as well. Holding this attitude at the centre of your negotiations will make you think and behave differently. It will increase respect, trust and rapport, and ultimately will produce better results for all. So, the first step of the negotiation is to prepare for this mental shift to take on a collaborative attitude and start working towards a situation where both of you can get more from the agreement.

We do this in three steps, our first three steps of negotiation, but first we begin to develop the collaborative mindset by thinking of *why* we want to cooperate to get this agreement in the first place. You need to be sure before you start to negotiate that you want to make an agreement, so that you can enter the negotiation as equals.

EQUALITY FIRST IN ACTION

One early spring day in 2005, I walked into a German motorcycle showroom in London to try to buy a new motorcycle. I had been riding this brand for a few years and was very excited about the new model that I had been reading about in the press but had rarely seen on the streets. I had called dealers up and down the country so I knew there was a waiting list for them, but I also knew that this specific dealer had a few arriving the next week. I was as well prepared as an expert on negotiation should be. I had worked out all the variables, created a 'Shopping List' (we'll come back to this idea in Chapter 3), and I even knew what I hoped to use as my negotiation tools. I had notes in my notebook, and I was full of confidence. The ride down had been clear, and I had cleaned my bike nicely at the jet wash en route, hoping to get the best deal I could on part exchange.

The salesman approached me with a confident welcome. We chatted for a while, and I told him why I wanted to talk about buying the new 1150R. However, remembering my grandmother's advice that 'enthusiasm is expensive', I let him know that I was considering some other options, and that I thought some of the extras were unnecessary and expensive. I didn't want him to feel I wanted the bike too much, as I thought he might take advantage of that knowledge. I explained that I just wanted to go through a few details with him and discuss the exact package that he could offer, and in doing so I probably gave away a little too much about my preparation. The fact I was clutching a little black book that I appeared to be referring to may have added to the impression that I felt he needed me more than I needed him.

As this salesman was clearly a professional, he asked me a simple question: 'Have you taken one for a test drive yet?'

I answered honestly 'No', but explained that I had read many reviews. His attitude shifted, and he leant back slightly and folded his arms.

'Well, I really am not comfortable talking to you about how we are going to sell you this bike, until you are 100 per cent sure that this is the bike you want to drive this summer. In fact, as I have a fully loaded version downstairs, I am going to insist you take a test drive before we discuss it any further.'

While I may have known what he was doing, I could appreciate where he was coming from too. As an avid biker, looking for what I thought could be the bike that I'd ride into my sunset years, and the first bike I'd buy brand new, I wanted to make sure I made the right choice too, so I accepted his offer.

I'm not sure if he had read my negotiation notes, or my mind, when he gave me a final heads-up before I took it out. I genuinely hadn't seen the point of spending £1,200 extra on ABS (anti-lock braking system), but I also knew that all the bikes on order were made with them fitted and they couldn't be removed. I was planning on making it an issue in our negotiation, and he was planning to neutralize it with his suggestion.

'Don't ride too fast in the park as there are speed cameras, but take it up to 30 on a straight line and pull the brakes hard, and see what happens. Then you can see whether ABS may be something that's worth adding to your bike.'

So I did as he suggested, and the effect was instant. I could see how amazing the braking was, and I was slightly disabled in my ability to argue that I didn't want ABS, because now I did.

What the salesman did here is not exceptional. He was doing what any salesperson should do before entering a negotiation. He was making sure that the sale was done first: that he was dealing with someone who actually wanted the bike in question before he started negotiating. He was ensuring that equality was present and that the conditions for win–win were met. He was trying to neutralize the attitude I had been giving him in mentioning the competitors that I was considering.

Not surprisingly, it worked ... to some extent. I came back with a grin on my face and an increased desire to do a deal on the day. He sensed this and started to shift his attitude too. As he eased himself into his chair and fired up his PC, he started to act like he really didn't need to sell a bike at all, like I needed to buy the bike more than he needed to sell it. And when he decided to tell me a lie to increase the desirability of the bike, the trust died. He wasn't looking for win–win, or equality. Fortunately, I was well prepared. An honest dealer had already shown me the screen he was looking at that enabled dealers to track orders at the BMW plant, so I knew what he was telling me wasn't entirely true.

I made my excuses and left. The truth was that this dealership had little emotional equity with me from past experiences, and it was all I needed to push me towards making a deal with someone else.

I tell the story here to illustrate three things that we should always do before negotiating. First, make sure both parties want to do a deal. Second, let them know that you know that. Third, think and act like you want to do best by the other party. This is the foundation for negotiations that create exceptional outcomes.

What we are looking for in our negotiations are extraordinary results. We are looking to create agreements

that add value for both parties, which means we are looking to find ways to give out more 'cookies' in the process.
For that reason, we are looking to adopt an attitude that
oozes cooperation. What happened in the motorbike
showroom is the opposite of this. We quickly became
positional, and instead of opening up to each other about
what was really true, we started playing games. I can take
responsibility because I came in intending to play the
'Reluctant Buyer' (see Chapter 12 on avoiding common
gambits), so I started things off on the wrong foot. When
the salesman started playing hard-to-get and exaggerat-
ing the low availability of the model, I could be sure that
collaboration wasn't on the cards, so I walked away.

By cooperating for win–win we create agreements
that work better for both parties as a result of our commitment to cooperate. We are trusting that if we pool
our resources and thinking, we can form an agreement
that creates more than it would have if we had tried to
outwit each other. Without understanding the central
importance of this attitude, reading any further is a waste
of time for you.

DISTINGUISHING BETWEEN SELLING AND NEGOTIATING

It's important to make sure you have completed the sales
process before you begin to negotiate. This is what any

good salesperson will do before talking money, and is what the motorcycle salesperson was attempting. If you don't have an agreement that the other person wants to do a deal with you, then you enter the discussion as an unequal party, and you will have to offer more than is reasonable to gain agreement. This is why it's critical before you talk about a deal to get agreement about the principle of doing a deal. Get agreement from the other party that they want to reach agreement and that they see value in the key elements you are discussing. In practical terms, this often means asking for agreement 'in principle'. Ensuring you have this agreement is critical for you to know that you are working towards an agreement that will work for both parties. The reason I insist on getting this agreement first is because without it, the whole process can become a theatrical performance that takes both parties further away from what they really want.

You must, therefore, determine whether the sales process has ended before you negotiate. How that looks in practice will depend on the agreement you are discussing, but in most cases it will involve the other party agreeing that they want to make a deal. Here's what it might look like in a few standard negotiation scenarios:

The estate agent will ask: 'Are you sure that this is the right house for you – before we start to speak to the seller about the details?'

The car dealer will ask, 'Are you happy that this car is right for your family?', before he talks about a package.

The mediator will ask a couple: 'Are you both willing to work together now to find an agreement that avoids you going through a legal process?'

The football player's agent may ask a prospective team: 'Are you sure that this player will fit into your current squad before I spend time working out a deal that is right for both the player and your club?'

try it now SECURING COMMITMENT TO NEGOTIATE

Imagine you are involved in a negotiation, or think about a real scenario from your life or business that will involve negotiating for mutual benefit. Think about the phrasing you will use to gain agreement to a deal 'in principle'. How will you ensure that the other party is committed in advance to negotiating with you? How will you build the idea of negotiating for mutual benefit into this part of the process? Write out a few examples, using the above samples as a guide, so you can become familiar with gaining agreement for mutually beneficial negotiations and collaborative processes.

Ask yourself: 'What could I do now to get my negotiation partner to openly acknowledge that we are both working positively towards a solution?' What phrase would you use, whether in person, on the phone or by email, to get them to state that? If you have a real negotiation in mind, go ahead and pick up the phone or email the person now. You will be surprised how much easier it becomes to negotiate if you are both agreed that you want a solution in the first place.

Before we start planning exactly what we need from a negotiation, it's worth understanding 'the why beneath the why', being crystal clear on your motive to make this agreement work. Having a collaborative attitude is key to this system, as anything else will lead to short-term gain and potential mistrust and will waste time and resources.

THE FOUR P'S – PRACTICAL QUESTIONS TO ASK BEFORE NEGOTIATING

A simple tool that I was taught by Sandra Proctor involves doing some practical research about your negotiation partner before moving forward. Sandra was one of my early mentors as a negotiator, and along with a gorgeous co-pilot, Nigel, ran negotiation training for the team at Capital Radio in the 1990s. I learned a huge amount from Sandra's workshops, which I have amended and adapted in my years as a trainer, including the importance of practising your negotiation strategies in all areas of your life. Her stories of how she applied what she called 'Win–Win Negotiation' in her personal and professional life demonstrated the principles' enormous potential for practical benefits. The tool is simple, a set of questions that get you thinking about *who* you are negotiating with, before you move on to the more practical issues you are facing.

Sandra refers to these questions – used to learn more about the person you're negotiating with – as the 'Four P's'.

1. PAST – What is their history, and what records can you check to see what deals they have done before?

2. PREFERENCES – What do they like, and, therefore, what variables may particularly appeal?

3. PREJUDICES – What don't they like, and, therefore, what variables may be off the table or not worth focusing on?

4. PERSONALITY – What are they like? What should we know about how they are as a person that will help us negotiate with them more effectively?

You could also think of the Four P's as the 'four likes'. What *were* they like? What *do* they like? What *don't* they like? What *are* they like? These are simple questions that will help you to understand what variables and processes may work best to secure a deal that suits everyone.

We will look at personality in some depth in Chapter 10, so at this stage it's just worth mentioning that clearly someone's personality will impact how they negotiate with you. I'm always reminded of my great uncle Benny, who used to run a jewellery business in London's Jewellery Quarter. He was famous in Hatton

Garden as a man who didn't haggle. If you brought something that you wanted him to buy, you'd have to offer a fair price as he'd consider that a last price and would simply say 'yes' or 'no'. Knowing that about Benny before going in to sell him a piece of jewellery would help you greatly.

try it now USING THE FOUR P'S

Think of your negotiation scenario from the previous exercise box. Ask these four questions about your real or imagined negotiation partner and make a note of your responses. Ask yourself, how will I use this information to craft a better deal for both of us?

SHIFTING ATTITUDES – CARING FIRST

Many years ago, while at university in Liverpool, I ran a small team of salespeople who rented out sunbeds to people's homes. As you may imagine, it was a relatively captive market, and people would pay around £20 a month to have a sunbed in their homes. We also sold sunbeds, but only to those who asked, as the rental market was where the money really was.

One month I hired a new caller, Gina, whose job was to call existing hirers and try to persuade them to extend their hire by giving them a small discount. It was a simple role, but one that yielded good returns, as we didn't need to go and get the bed back and redeliver it somewhere else. Gina was one of the warmest and most empathetic people, and within moments on the phone she would be chatting to strangers about all sorts. At first I was a little irritated and concerned by the length of time she spent on calls. However, although her call rates were low, I could see that her results were much better than everyone else's in her team. She was building a level of trust that enabled people to want to do a deal with her, and often at a much lesser discount than our average.

One day she turned to me and suggested a brilliant plan to create a hire purchase scheme/loyalty club that was absolutely win–win for everyone involved. Not only did it become a great seller, but the customer to whom Gina had been talking who had actually suggested the idea resold twelve of the packages to members of her wider family. Gina taught us about the power of patience in customer relationships; if you take the time to really understand what people need, you will be able to produce tailored packages that add value to both sides.

THINK 'WE, THEN ME'

The final piece of mental preparation for collaborative negotiation involves understanding the importance of 'we, then me'. See that you can achieve more by collaborating with a negotiation partner than you can achieve apart. It is important to realize before we go into the practical preparation that we are aiming to achieve something greater from our collaboration than we are likely to achieve on our own. In this way, we are not putting our own interests second, but rather we are recognizing that our own interests are best served as part of an agreement with the other party. Until we find a common interest, our personal interests are unlikely to be furthered significantly. When we see that the other party can bring ideas and strategies to the table that can strengthen our personal position, only then can we really negotiate collaboratively.

This goes beyond the merely practical element behind the expression 'two heads are better than one', although as Steven Smith, author and co-founder of G5 Leadership, points out in his book *Catalyst*, while nineteen individuals won the first fifteen Nobel Prizes in Physics, over the past fifteen years the Prize has gone to 42 people. The ability to collaborate effectively has become critical, not just in business but in science too. Smith also points us to a landmark study of 3,000 married couples, conducted by the psychologist John Gottman. Gottman discovered that couples who are collaborative stand a greater chance of staying together and of achieving more in their lives together. Yet beyond that simple short-term success, there seems to be another reason in our socially networked world why the ability to collaborate and work effectively with others is vital. Smith writes:

The interactive, social world is where confidence and competence connect to produce relevance: where what I can do meets what you need. The tighter the connection, the stronger the relevance. As relevance goes, confidence and competence often follow.

case study
SIMON'S PITCH FOR A MARKETING CONTRACT

In Chapter 1, we introduced the story of Kathleen, negotiating for a job as Commercial Director of her company. We'll come back to Kathleen in Chapter 3, but for now will look at applying the tools from Chapter 2 to a design business that provides services to the financial sector. They are a team of ten, and they have just won the pitch for a major bank to create 'collateral' (brochures, posters and online materials) for a new type of savings account for 'tweenagers'.

At this stage, we know that everyone wants to do the deal; now it's down to Simon, the Managing Director, to negotiate the deal with Luca, the local Marketing Lead for the bank. The issue is complicated by the fact that the deal will need to go through a 'procurement' team at the bank, who are professional negotiators whose job is to ensure that everything bought for the bank is done so with the best terms possible.

Using the checklist on page 38, Simon can ask himself what he knows about both the people he is working with specifically and the organization more broadly (the Four P's). He discovers that while he has done work for the bank before in different areas, he doesn't know enough. So he calls people he does know to get more information. He discovers that his contacts can fill him in on aspects of the Marketing Lead's *Personality* – discovering that Luca is particularly analytical and detail-focused

– and also on the issues they have had in the *Past* in having to deliver detailed timelines on projects and spend extra time presenting and monitoring these project plans. He discovers that some of the bank's other agencies hot-desk (*Preferences*) and learns a lot more about why the incumbent agency wasn't meeting their needs around reporting and delivering digital file back-ups (*Prejudices*).

In developing a better understanding of key contact Luca, how he likes to work, and what had really got in the way of previous relationships, Simon can see what is important to the Marketing Lead (detail, careful project planning and a focus on having an hourly rate that meets a bank 'standard'). Importantly, he also knows what isn't so important to Luca and what can be leveraged (project planning) to make the deal more attractive – to the bank.

Armed with all this information, Simon is more confident he can craft an agreement that not only produces great work, but does it in a way that will work for the bank, and for his business. His major insight is that while he will have to agree a standard hourly rate for design, he will be able to include other 'chargeable items' that will add value for his business and enable his team to work harder and more creatively for the bank.

This initial preparation informs Simon that he wants to do a deal and to create a long-term relationship with the bank (questions 1 and 4 in the checklist). He can also see from his discussions with various bank employees that they are looking for an agency to create a long-term partnership with.

Work through the questions in the checklist for yourself. What can you learn from Simon that may make you better prepared for your next negotiation?

CHECKLIST FOR MENTAL PREPARATION

1. Do you really want to do this deal?

2. Are you sure the other party wants to do a deal, and if so have they expressed that desire to you?

3. Do you feel equal and working towards a solution that is mutually beneficial?

4. Do you want to have a long-term relationship with the person you are negotiating with?

5. What can you do to ensure the other party is committed to working towards a solution that produces benefit for all parties?

6. How can you get them to openly express the desire for a mutually agreeable solution, either to you or in public?

7. Do you know what they like? (Preferences)

8. Do you know what they don't like? (Prejudices)

9. Do you have any research into their past agreements that you can use to inform this agreement? (Past)

10. What do you know about their personality? (Personality)

CHAPTER 3

Step Two – Preparing a Plan

Chance favours the prepared mind.

Louis Pasteur

Once we have a collaborative mindset and have done our best to ensure we have a partner on the same page, we can set about preparing to make deals that work for all. In this chapter we will explore the steps you will take to make sure you are ready to move on and discuss the next steps with your partner.

UNDERSTANDING THE POWER OF VARIABLES

One of the key messages of this book is that negotiation is simple. All we are looking to do is craft agreements with other humans that get more. More for us and more for them. The tools that we use to access this are variables: options that enable win–win.

A 'variable' is no more than any factor that can change in our negotiation and that may help to get agreement. It's a 'variable' because it's something that can vary. Academics often compare these to 'constants', those elements of a negotiation that are fixed, or can't change in the negotiation. The truth is that very little is constant in most of the negotiations, but the idea is valid. Let's say you are negotiating over a car; the car is the constant. But enough of the academics of negotiation, let's work out what kind of variables are key to successful outcomes.

Variables are the things that add value to one or the other party as part of a deal, and good variables will have a magical quality to them. That is, a good variable adds balance in one person's favour without costing the other too much. Remember how Millie found a cookie to trade in the story from the opening chapter? That was the 'ah-ha moment' that moved us on and enabled us to collaborate. We found something that was high value to her and cost me nothing. It's easy for me to trade it with her to get what I want.

Roger Fisher, the Harvard professor who co-wrote the classic negotiation text *Getting to Yes*, called this hunt for good variables 'searching for creative options', and it's this creativity that, in my experience, makes outstanding negotiators. How well can you work before and during the negotiation to generate a list of variables that will be high value to the other party and not cost you too much to deliver? What things can you deliver at low cost that would cost more in time, money or effort for the other party to get?

I'll give you an example. My wife runs a 'glamping' business which puts up luxury tents at festivals. One of the variables she uses if people are looking to get a special deal is a bottle of chilled champagne. This is something that would cost over £60 to buy at a festival, and bringing one yourself isn't really possible because glass is rarely permitted on site. For my wife, it's easy to procure, and she disposes of the bottles herself (as she brings a large van to the site, that's easy for her). During the year, as she does her weekly shopping, she picks up cases of champagne at very low prices from supermarkets when they are on special. Her customers get to enjoy a bottle of champagne, which never costs her more than £15.

This is an example of a great variable because it's low cost to her and high value to the recipient. The other reason it's a great variable is because it's a real win–win. Not only is it cheap for her and valuable to them, it also meets a business need. She wants her customers to have a good time, that's part of what she is offering as a proposition. And we all know, for many festival goers, a bottle of champagne is an easy way to achieve that!

Let's look at another example. Take the experience of being upgraded to 'Premium Economy' on Virgin Atlantic. In itself 'upgrading' is a great variable for any airline to use, because when they have space, it's low cost to them and it has a high perceived value to the passenger. The whole experience is packed with small low-cost variables that add value and work towards a better outcome for both parties. One is the bottle of water they give as passengers arrive in the cabin, low cost to them (probably no more than 20p), but adding a layer of perceived value to the traveller, who has just come out of an airport lounge where the cheapest bottle of water you could buy is £1.75.

It gets better, as the water Virgin offer is One Water, a brand that gives its profits to sustainable water development charities. So, not only do the aeroplane staff receive fewer requests for water, but Virgin's brand is enhanced by its association with One. Three parties get something from this variable (the passenger, Virgin and One). And all for 20p.

Being creative with inventing and using variables is key to successful negotiations. When I work with advertising sales teams, it's amazing how many have limited themselves to what they can include in a deal. When we brainstorm potential variables, possibilities expand, and the potential for better outcomes for both parties instantly increases.

So, part of your preparation is to start thinking creatively about what variables you can use that are low cost to you and high value to the other party. Doing step one – preparing yourself mentally and thinking win–win – will have helped in this. Understanding their needs and what they want from the deal is critical to finding variables that will craft great agreements. The attitude that is required here is *abundance*: what could I give that will add value? Remember, at this stage you are not giving it, just preparing for what may add value to this deal.

One of my favourite exercises in my company, Inspire's, training programmes is when we brainstorm variables to try to think of as many possible options that we can include in future deals. What we often discover during these exercises is that there are more variables in many deals than you would have imagined before beginning your preparation. When selling your house or car there may be obvious extras that can be added or taken away – the inclusion of white goods in the house, or higher-quality upholstery in the car – yet other deals may require you to stretch your imagination. Can you find good variables that add value to one party, while not costing too much for the other side?

The following case studies explore this creative variable brainstorming process in two very different businesses.

case study
DENTAL SALES AND CUSTOMER-FOCUSED DEALS

Robin works in dental equipment sales and has an interesting challenge. As much of the equipment he sells are expensive, big-ticket items, his contacts are often at quite a high level, such as owner-operators at the head of large dental chains. Robin represents a premium manufacturer and has been in the business for a while, so he has good contacts and high rapport with them. His company, however, also relies on selling lower level consumables to a different client base: people at a local level, such as practice managers or administrative assistants. These clients have relationships with multiple suppliers and are often more focused on short-term ordering, delivery and personal incentives.

Robin realized that what he needed were introductions and regular meetings with these people in order to boost that side of his business. He also realized, in speaking with his customers, that they would like to see more competitive and keener long-term pricing, as well as more flexible invoicing to keep cash flow in the right place. As his business doesn't have an issue with cash flow, and has many customers in other medical markets that pay on longer terms, Robin saw opportunity to add valuable variables to his deals. The agreements he started to craft began to make a real difference to his business and the practices he serves. One variable he asks for is a regular monthly meeting with the local practice manager. He says he's only ever once been denied it when mandated as part of the larger deal, and it has led to better relationships and more mutually agreeable deals.

case study
WEDDING PHOTOGRAPHY AND FLEXIBLE PACKAGES

My wedding photographer had a very interesting approach to using variables. He had created a large number of variables that he was able to use to build a package that created value for all the parties involved. With variables like the length of time he was with us, the number of photos he would take, the materials he would use in the printing and binding of the photos, and the speed with which he would get the pictures online, there were a number of options we could add or take away.

Many of the options were clearly easy for him to deliver, like staying at the venue until the final dance, or making the photos available to guests online the very next day, but as they were hard for us to do ourselves, and thus valuable to us, it felt like it was win–win, as we created a package that worked for the whole family, which included albums for our parents, and access to the photos for everyone else.

Next time you are preparing for a negotiation, think about creating as large a list as possible of variables that will add value to the deal; the larger the list, the more likely you are to get a win–win deal. Start by thinking of all the things that you could add to the agreement that may be low cost to you but could be high value to the other party. Think as widely as you can. There is nothing that is out of bounds in your thinking here; as long as you could include it as part of your discussion and bargaining, you can make it a variable. If you find you don't have a good enough understanding of your partner to come up with a lot of variables, go back to your Four P's and do some more preparation about their preferences and needs.

THE VALUE OF A COMPLETE 'SHOPPING LIST'

A simple tool that will help you create more collaborative deals is what I call a 'Shopping List'. This is a list of the variables you think you can use to add value for yourself or the other party. The more complete this list you make now, the more options you will have when you are negotiating your deals. This is a resource you will be using throughout the process, so putting time into it now will help you later. Remember, this list is just the starting point, a place to go to throughout the negotiation when you need ideas to move your agreement forward.

try it now   CREATING YOUR SHOPPING LIST

Think about the negotiation you've been looking at over several exercises in the book thus far.

First, list all the fixed items that you are not willing to negotiate on. Be sure that these really are fixed. These are your 'constants'.

Now make a list of at least ten different ways you could vary the agreement. Think about timescales, services and added values. Think about the things you can do to support the agreement. Think as broadly as possible, and make your list a little longer. Mark any of the variables which are 'Superstar Variables', that is the ones that are very low cost to you, but extra high value to the other party. These are the ones that will bring most extra value to the deal. Remember, you will need to check these assumptions about value in your discussion with the other party, but you have made a good start here.

Think about which items you could ask for that would be good variables from the other party's perspective. What can they offer you that will be low cost to them and high value to you?

A couple of years ago, my son Ziggy, who was seven at the time, turned to me while watching the band One Direction at Capital Radio's Jingle Bell Ball. 'I can't believe this is happening to me,' he said, expressing his complete amazement at being so close to his heroes as they sang one of his favourite songs. He was in awe, and it was a heart-warming moment for me. Getting to the concert was the direct result of doing the Shopping List exercise a few months before. In negotiating a deal with a regular customer, Global Radio, I had thought about what might be low cost to them and high value to me. Tickets to the ball had popped into my mind, and I realized it would be easy for my contact to make that happen, but it added an immeasurable value for me, beyond anything money could buy.

If we fail to look creatively for added value in agreements, then we miss an opportunity to make every agreement more valuable. This is a key tool in negotiation, and the more you practise using it, the better the deals you will make.

USING THE THREE-STEP WIN MATRIX

Another very practical tool in preparing for a negotiation is your three-step WIN Matrix. This is simply a place where you record what you WANT, what you INTEND and what you NEED from the agreement. It is what's often referred to as your 'Top', 'Middle' and 'Bottom' Lines. Thinking about the matrix now will help you to craft an agreement that sits comfortably with you and your partner later.

You will usually have a key variable (often price or time) that you know will form the centre of your agreement. Using one of these key variables, think about what your highest and lowest expectations are and write them down as your Top and Bottom Lines; in your Middle Line space, put the number you would most expect to settle for. Let's say your key variable is time, and your Want/Top Line is to get the project completed in four months. Your Need/Bottom Line is ten months, and your Intent/Middle Line that you expect will be the agreed timescale is seven months.

Now, around these three figures you can group other variables that you think will be appropriate to add or take away if you move to that level. So, perhaps you would be happy to increase the price to move the timescale up to your Top Line level, or you would only go down to your Bottom Line level if you secured additional services.

It is a good idea to do this exercise on paper, creating three distinct sections on the page for each step in the WIN Matrix. So many times I have seen people discuss this process in simulations, only to fail to record it. What happens afterwards, especially in group situations, is predictable. Disagreement, confusion and missed expectations.

When we did this as a team in one of the commercial operations I worked with, we instantly saw a measurable increase in two critical areas: the availability of the most sought-after products and the yield produced for the total of the inventory. Just by producing WIN Matrices (and discussing this as teams), the business put the focus on to the variables that really mattered. Results in these areas followed almost instantly. I would challenge anyone to do this exercise carefully and not feel an increase in your confidence and competence as a negotiator.

The important thing is to record the three steps or three key measurables for a successful outcome – your Top, Middle and Bottom Lines – and to test for yourself which variables may work at each level. Record these measurables so that you can easily talk to any other stakeholders in the deal and discuss your thinking rationally with them. Often just by doing the exercise and talking it through with someone else you will get better ideas about how you can structure a deal that works best for both parties – especially when you agree the key variables, the possible additional variables and your Bottom Line.

try it now PREPARE FOR A REAL NEGOTIATION AND CREATE YOUR WIN MATRICES

You might want to buy yourself a special notebook in which to do your negotiation preparations. I enjoy having a small book that I can carry with me to record my thinking and add any thoughts as they appear in the moment.

In this book, or on a piece of paper, mark three imaginary lines, a top, middle and bottom, creating a WIN Matrix for an agreement you are looking to create. Using your Shopping List of variables from the previous exercise, add some ideas around the three lines, and start to visualize how a satisfactory outcome may look to you.

Remember, you will be doing this from your partner's perspective in the next stage, so leave their expectations and variables aside for the time being.

RED LINES AND WALKING AWAY

The need for a clear 'Red Line' is absolute in effective negotiations. The Red Line is the lowest point you can go to in order to conclude an agreement; it is a line that you will not cross to get a deal. Beyond this point you would have to walk away if the other party couldn't meet your requirements. While often this is a question of finance, there may be other Red Lines that you realize are key to a successful agreement. Not being clear about this Red Line, or 'walk-away point', is an easy way to get to deals that don't work for either party. However, if you are clear about what your Red Lines are, you will be a more confident and clearer negotiator.

case study GETTING WHAT YOU NEED FROM A DEAL

Jon works for a charity, which recently faced a crisis with one of its key staff members. The fate of the whole project was in the balance over a small salary issue. When the dust had finally settled and they were back on track, Jon and the member of staff took a walk in the woods and the member of staff confided in him. She had been so eager to take the job in the first place, and the organization had been so clear about its salary expectations, that she hadn't really prepared for the salary negotiation. She had accepted an offer that was below what she had expected to be offered, but also below what she really needed. While she wanted to work, what it meant was that she had to work in a second job to support her family. The charity wasn't getting all it could from her, and she wasn't getting all she needed. Better preparation and more effective discussion could have created a more collaborative agreement that would have worked better for both.

try it now TESTING YOUR WALK-AWAY POINT

It is a good idea to test your Red Line, by asking the question: 'Would I accept a little lower?' If your answer is 'yes', then that new figure is your real Red Line. It's best to be honest with yourself now, so you can be happier with the final outcome.

OTHER OPTIONS – IS THERE AN ALTERNATIVE TO DOING THIS DEAL?

A good negotiator is always prepared to walk away from a proposed deal if it doesn't make sense for both parties. This is critical, and it's important that you think about it carefully. Thinking about what the alternative to doing the deal is will help focus you on what your Red Line should really be. In the language of Harvard Business School, this is called a Best Alternative To a Negotiated Agreement (BATNA). Their research points to the fact that having a BATNA adds confidence and conviction to a negotiator during their negotiations. They also find it helps both parties understand the value of doing a deal, knowing that there is a viable alternative to not doing one. This can often be a difficult thing to accept if you have put a lot into getting this far in the process, but it's critical nonetheless.

It's therefore helpful to list what you will do if you don't reach a deal with this person or company right now. The need for an alternative is not only to help your confidence though, it's practical. Unless you know what the alternative is to making an agreement, you won't be able to calculate the cost of not doing the deal. Say you are going to negotiate for a car, and you have planned your Red Line on the price. What is your plan if the seller won't sell above that line? Have you got a rental option or a car to borrow? If you are negotiating for a job, what will you do if you can't reach an agreement? Will you pull out of the hiring process? Are there other opportunities you can pursue? Having a next best option in your mind, and knowing what you can or cannot concede in order to make a deal happen, will help you negotiate with confidence and clarity.

I recently consulted around a family dispute between a mother and some of her children. We soon realized something quite profound when we got to this point. There was no walk-away point; there could be no clear Red Line. She wasn't walking away, and so what we were looking at wasn't really a negotiation, more a mediation, where you work towards finding the best ways to disagree. If that is your situation, then this kind of preparation won't necessarily work for you. You can only negotiate with someone as their equal, and if you are always going to accept any offer that is made, then you are not really negotiating at all. For more on navigating the complexities of negotiating with family, see Chapter 11.

case study KATHLEEN'S WIN MATRIX

Kathleen writes out a set of WIN outcomes for herself, so that she has a clear idea of her Top, Middle and Bottom Lines. In her case, these outcomes are largely focused on salary. She knows how much value she can bring to the company, and has done her research on what she could earn at other companies using her skill-set. So, in her Top Line, she puts an ambitious, ideal salary; in her Middle Line she puts a solid salary increase that she would be happy to take; in her Bottom Line she puts a salary that would meet her needs and that she would accept only in exchange for other variables.

Around this core issue, she also has a number of other variables, like share options, holiday allowance, a company car and healthcare. Depending on the company's preferences for paying greater salaries with lower benefits or vice versa, Kathleen can negotiate a package that meets her needs while also being viable for her employer. Writing this out is valuable because it enables her to think about which variables will be low cost for the company but high value for her (a higher-quality company car), as well as which variables would be walk-away points (lack of flexible hours, such that she couldn't pick her kids up from nursery twice a week).

Kathleen can now go into a discussion with a clear idea of her expected outcomes, and enough flexibility to craft an agreement that meets her needs and wants while also meeting her company's needs and wants. However, she still needs to do a bit more work to understand what will really add value for her company in order to craft the best long-term agreement for all.

case study SIMON'S WIN MATRIX

The number of variables Simon has to play with is large, so Simon asks his team to list them all in a brainstorm to help him prepare. They include cloud-based storage solutions that are low cost to Simon, an online collaboration tool and project planning monitoring, a dedicated project manager to report weekly on the project, designers working on-site at the bank for three days a week, a daily or weekly 'online huddle' (project update meetings), dedicated designers for the bank, and access to design resource databases the agency uses for the bank's marketing team.

Simon focuses on creating his Top, Middle and Bottom Lines based on hourly rates and monthly retainers. Having a clear Bottom Line in terms of rate and retainer that he is able to test as reasonable with others affords him the confidence and clarity to work more creatively with the list of variables his team has helped create. His WIN outcomes are focused on the hourly rate and volumes, but he sees that different variables will be appropriate at different levels. At a high-volume guarantee and high rates, he sees that he could provide a dedicated project manager on the account, plus daily huddles, and people working on-site at the bank more regularly. As the volume commitment reduces (his Middle Line, or Intent), he sees that he would have to offer fewer dedicated workers and less regular reporting. Once he gets close to his Need, or Bottom Line, in terms of rate and commitment, he would not be able to provide cloud solutions without extra cost, nor online collaboration tools for the whole team.

CHECKLIST FOR EFFECTIVE PREPARATION

1. Have you considered what the best variables are that may add value to the other party?

2. Have you considered what variables you may ask for from the other party that may add value to you but not cost them too much?

3. Have you listed your WIN Matrix: Want, Intend, Need (your Top, Middle and Bottom Lines)?

4. Are you certain that your Need is actually a Red Line?

5. Have you considered what you will do if you don't get a deal?

6. Are you feeling comfortable that you have enough variables to work with that you can produce an agreement that works for both parties?

CHAPTER 4

Step Three –
Understanding Your
Partner's Point of View

Seek first to understand, then to be understood.

Stephen Covey

It is a simple idea, and yet in my experience this is the most powerful step of this system: only when you really understand where the other person is coming from can you genuinely craft an agreement that works for both parties. In this vital, final stage of preparation, you prepare to collaborate by going through the same process that you just went through for yourself, but you do it from your partner's perspective. You literally take their point of view, in order to understand how you can get an agreement that will really work for them.

One of the challenges of seeing another person's point of view is that it is hard to see from two places at the same time. My father used to quote one of his teachers, who told him: 'If you want to walk in someone else's shoes, you first need to take off your own.' So, remember that the first part of this exercise will be trying to let go of your own perspective for a while.

UNDERSTANDING YOUR GREEN ZONES OF AGREEMENT

In this stage of preparation we start to work out how big our 'Green Zone of Agreement' really is, or how much margin for agreement we really have. Picturing this Zone of Agreement is useful in order to work out what you will need to do to create a deal that satisfies both parties, and promotes future collaboration. What you soon realize when you look at the picture from the other person's perspective is what you will really have to do to get an agreement that works.

In highly charged situations, seeing the other party's point of view is critical; it's why hostage negotiators will do as much research as they possibly can into the person they are negotiating with. They will analyse everything they can about that person, so they can see where they're coming from, and foresee their next move. As one of the key objectives of any negotiator in a crisis is to calm the hostage taker's emotional state, one of the primary tools they use is to build empathy and rapport by trying to show that they understand the other person's point of view.

Let's start trying to do this in a work scenario. Using the same tools you used in the previous chapter, walk through the process as if you were the other person, and make a list of what you want to make the agreement work most effectively. In order to do this, use the information you gained in the first stage. Think about how they got to the place they are in, what is driving them forward, and what may be holding them back. One very powerful way to do this is to imagine yourself stepping into their actual body for a while and, from their perspective, to do the preparation of creating a list of variables, a Top, Middle and Bottom Line, and clear Red Lines, or walk-away points.

THINK ABOUT IT: WHAT PERSPECTIVE ARE YOU SEEING CLEARLY?

A few years ago, I came to a realization about perspectives while staying with my brother, Dylan, in Washington, DC. He married an American and works for the US government, so, despite being born in the UK, he's now a fully naturalized American.

I challenged him about a world map he had on the wall, which placed America in the centre. I was looking at it from my perspective, and it seemed odd to me because it was not what I was used to. So, I saw it as an example of the United States' insular nature, that Americans would reengineer a global map to make themselves look more important. As Dylan took me around his house, showing me different maps of the world, created from different perspectives (he's a bit of a cartographer on the side), it suddenly struck me that my view of what constituted the 'right' map just came from the way I had always seen it: with Britain in the centre. The words of Stephen Covey rang in my ears: 'We don't see the world as it is, but as we are.'

> Understanding how your negotiation partner sees the world, and recognizing that it might differ from your own point of view, is vital if you are to understand how you can come up with a mutually agreeable solution.

NLP (neurolinguistic programming) is a personal development theory that has been used by many businesses in their training and development programmes. Developed in the 1980s by Richard Bandler and John Grinder, NLP teaches an understanding of how the brain ('neuro') processes information and language ('linguistics') to create behaviour ('programming'). The founders and other practitioners use models of effective behaviour around which they create processes that people can use to change their attitudes and actions.

One of these models is a very powerful process called 'Deep Trance Identification'. In the process you are taken, or you take yourself, into a deep state of relaxation, or hypnotic trance. From that place you imagine a person you want to learn from, making a very clear picture of them in your mind. Using a number of mental triggers, you create a powerful image of them, complete with pictures, sounds, feelings, smells and even tastes. Once this picture is complete, you step into the person's body and imagine yourself as that person. Many people experience quite amazing insights using this process. They feel themselves tapping into the wisdom of people far away from them, sometimes people they have never met. While Deep Trance Identification may sound all a little eccentric to you, my Grandma, who would have had no time for it at all under this name, used to tell me that she would often imagine what her father would do, when she was faced with a difficult challenge. So, we are not talking about anything much more profound than my Grandma's wisdom.

try it now IDENTIFICATION EXERCISE

The purpose of this exercise is to see the world through the eyes of the person you are negotiating with, by thinking of the five senses and providing your brain with specific information to build a mental image of this person. More than that, you will also *feel* the world through their body, and *hear* the world through their ears.

Take a moment to relax and clear your mind. Take five deep breaths and bring your attention to the moment. Then imagine a person you are trying to create an agreement with. Imagine them standing or sitting in front of you. How do they hold themselves? How are they breathing? What are they feeling as they prepare to talk to you about this agreement? You can use any kind of triggers: visual (such as what they're wearing, their hair and eye colour), kinaesthetic (the feelings, movements or gestures you associate with this person), auditory (the sound of their voice, other noises in the room), olfactory (the perfume they wear or the smell of coffee on their breath) or even gustatory (what they've had to eat) to imagine what their world is like.

Once you have a clear picture of them in your mind, visualize yourself stepping into their physical body and taking over their world. Imagine how it feels to be them, sitting or standing in their own space, thinking through making an agreement with you. Whether you do this with your eyes closed or not is irrelevant.

Experience this for a moment before you prepare using the three-step WIN Matrix that we introduced in Chapter 3. You should end up with the same output as in your own preparation. You should have a clear understanding of what you think your partner's Top, Middle and Bottom Lines are, and what you think their Red Lines will be, those points which they feel they cannot go below for any variables. As in your own preparation, you should have created a list of key variables: things that are low cost to your partner and high value to you that you may be able to trade to get an agreement that works well. Armed with this list of ideal variables for your partner, and ideal variables for you, you'll start to see those Green Zones of Agreement, where your interests overlap.

CREATING GREEN ZONES OF AGREEMENT

Essentially, we are looking to make sure there is enough space between what we want and what the other person wants to get some kind of agreement. We can summarize the whole negation process as:

$$\text{Negotiation} = \frac{\text{Their Needs}}{\text{Your Needs}}$$

I like to call this the 'Green Zone of Agreement'. It is also sometimes referred to as the 'ZOPA' (Zone of Possible Agreement). Part of our job as negotiators is to make this zone as wide and as fertile as possible. We do this by focusing on areas where we have mutual benefit and we can see agreement. The more carefully we delve into our partner's needs, the more we are likely to find areas of agreement, and create ideas that will pull us away from conflict.

It's important to realize that it's not just by using our rational or analytical thinking that we will find areas of agreement. In *Thinking Fast and Slow*, Daniel Kahneman, a Nobel Prize-winning psychologist and behavioural economist, points to the opposite. He suggests that our *intuitive* thinking is far more likely to find creative solutions than our rational mind. Sometimes allowing ourselves to ask 'what if?', rather than 'what is?', provides a route to new ideas and a more fertile Green Zone. In my seminars, it is easy to see this phenomenon at work. I ask two teams to negotiate a simulated industrial dispute, giving exactly the same brief to both groups. But I ask one team to do the job very seriously and stress the importance of doing it right and getting the process right. The other team I instruct to enjoy the process and do their best to reach an agreement that benefits both parties. The results often vary dramatically. More often than not, the team that takes the job seriously misses out on the more creative act of brainstorming possible outcomes and looking for a Green Zone. Focused on 'getting it right', their analytical minds go into overload, and they focus on numbers over ideas. The team instructed to enjoy the process invariably comes up with more ideas, more questions and a greater likelihood of a collaborative discussion that creates ground for agreement.

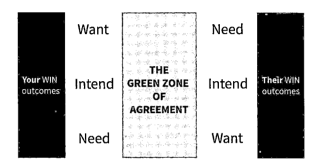

try it now FINDING YOUR GREEN ZONE

Thinking about a specific agreement you'd like to make, list your Top, Middle and Bottom Lines on the left side of a piece of paper. Next to each section, write the variables you'd like to propose to make the deal work best. On the right-hand side of the sheet, list your partner's Top, Middle and Bottom Lines as you have imagined them, or are imagining them now. To the left of that write the key variables that will be low cost for them to trade and could add value to you. Look carefully at what you have in front of you.

I can remember the first time I developed a WIN Matrix for my negotiation partner and looked at the Green Zone for our upcoming negotiation, and the impact it had. I was negotiating an advertising contract on behalf of a radio group with a growing media agency. As a sales team, we were very clear about our targets and yield expectations, and we were clear about what we needed from our customers. I had created my own Top, Middle and Bottom Lines based on those expectations and the rates the advertiser had used on the last piece of business they did (which was a short-term deal). I knew my Red Line, and I knew the kind of variables I could use that would be high value to my partners and those that would be low value to them.

When I looked at my matrix from their point of view, though, I got a bit of a shock. My picture looked distorted. Thinking about the actual person in the agency made me think about the rates they currently paid on other pieces of business. I also started to think of what they really wanted to achieve in terms of keeping this client happy and keeping their bosses happy. I realized quickly that our Green Zone was very thin. There was little space between our Red Lines. Some of the variables which I had thought of seemed irrelevant alongside their objectives, and it seemed like if I was going to get agreement I would have to work hard, either to shift their expectations or the expectations of my team.

The insight it gave me enabled me to sit down with my Sales Director and think carefully about different approaches that might produce an outcome that would work better for all of us. What we came up with were

Ask yourself the same question about your own expectations. Make sure you are creating expectations that are not mutually exclusive: it should be possible to achieve both outcomes if you can find suitable terms that balance these expectations.

Ask yourself: 'What would need to happen to make this a reality?' Thinking with this mindset, being patient and waiting for solutions to come to you will create exceptional results if you allow it.

case study

KATHLEEN'S STORY: FINDING AREAS OF AGREEMENT

Kathleen's research shows her that there is a good Green Zone between her and the company's salary expectations, partly because the other candidate would be effectively stepping down into the role, from being the Managing Partner of a successful, 'boutique' agency.

She can also see, however, by speaking to the departing CD, that some of her ideas around working flexibly have been rejected in the past. She decides to keep them on her list, and takes the opportunity to discuss with the HR Director her attitude to working from home before she accepts what she had been told is a Red Line for her business. What are the company's concerns motivating this Red Line – have these privileges been abused by other employees in the past, or are they worried it will diminish the face-time she can offer her team? Understanding these concerns allows Kathleen to address them specifically and turn a Red Line into something that can add value instead. She suggests scheduling in video calls with her team throughout her work-from-home days, and offers to share her personal schedule such that her team knows when she will be out of contact.

This also enables Kathleen to diminish the effect that flexible working has on the other variables in her negotiation: if it is no longer a big Red Line for the company, she doesn't have to offer a big sacrifice in salary or holiday expectations in order to keep this variable in the deal.

CHECKLIST FOR PREPARING FROM YOUR PARTNER'S POINT OF VIEW

1. Have you seen, and do you understand, your partner's point of view?

2. Have you listed their Top, Middle and Bottom Lines? Are you clear of their Red Lines?

3. Do you have a list of variables that are most likely to be on their Shopping List?

4. Have you understood how big your Green Zone really is? Can you see enough in this zone for agreement? Bear in mind that the larger this area, the more likely you are to make an agreement that works for all.

5. Have you thought about what would wildly exceed their expectations? And what would wildly exceed yours?

CHAPTER 5

Step Four – Discussing

In order to craft an agreement that genuinely benefits both parties, you will need to sit down first with whoever you are negotiating with and discuss all the issues frankly. At this point, bear in mind that not all of the people you negotiate with will be familiar with the principles of collaborative negotiation, so you will need to use this discussion to open them up to the increased possibilities that come with collaboration. Ideally, this is done face-to-face, but sometimes a phone call may be your only practical option. Use this discussion as your opportunity to really find out what will make this deal work best for all the parties involved. How you structure and lead this discussion will directly impact how easy it will be for you to collaborate.

At the heart of any discussion around a negotiated agreement is a collaborative mindset and a willingness to seek an agreement that works for all. Sir Paul Getty, the philanthropist and son of American industrialist Jean Paul Getty, quotes his father on developing this mindset:

> *You must never try to make all the money that is in a deal. Let the other fellow make some money too, because if*

you have a reputation for always making all the money,
you won't have many deals.

Getty understood the importance of this willingness to collaborate when we are discussing with another party what we want to achieve from a negotiation. Two skills are critical to any discussion – questioning and listening – and a collaborative attitude underpins them both. A collaborative attitude requires you to be open to listening to things you may not want to hear, and to be willing to share your position, so that the other parties understand your point of view.

In international conflict resolution, much emphasis is understandably placed on the discussion stage of the negotiations. Preliminary discussion to tease out the issues can often last for days, and is often where much of the most important work takes place. In this stage, we put all of our hard work from the preparation stages into play, providing ourselves with an opportunity to test all of our theories and expectations. It's important to be careful about how we manage this stage, as we are now face-to-face with the other party, and everything we say and ask is likely to be interpreted as what we are expecting as part of the final outcome.

I strongly recommend that you are clear and open at this stage, and that you are explicit about your intention to negotiate collaboratively. If you share your intention with your partner, you will build trust, accelerate rapport, and lubricate the whole process. Bear in mind that if you are negotiating with someone who doesn't share your approach, you may need to adjust your strategy and be less collaborative. My experience is that most people really understand the value of collaboration, but they do need to be reminded of it, especially in situations where they feel a lot is at stake. Explain your views, highlight the long–term impact for them and genuinely express your desire to create an outcome that works best for all parties.

try it now STATING YOUR INTENTION TO COLLABORATE

Write down in your notebook a phrase that expresses your intention to work collaboratively, a phrase that makes your attitude to negotiation clear. Ask yourself if it sounds clear and inspiring, enough that you would use it to introduce the idea to the other party before you discuss your options. If you can't articulate the idea on paper now, make sure you come back to this exercise again. Being able to clearly articulate your desire to work together for a mutual gain is critical to making the discussion phase valuable in your negotiations.

For instance, you might write:

'I know it's important for both of us to reach an agreement that works today.'

'I really want to make sure we can find a way to make this work for all of us.'

'I know we both want to negotiate a deal that makes sense to all of us.'

THE POWER OF *IF*

It is important that when we enter the discussion phase of any negotiation we are careful with our words. We do not want to imply anything through our questioning, or infer anything in our listening, that sets unreasonable expectations in the other party or ourselves. Therefore, we should ensure that our language is very *conditional* when we are making suggestions or presenting ideas – that everything we suggest is provisional and attached to agreement on other variables. The word 'if' is a useful aid in this stage. You should use it wisely in order to make sure that everything that you suggest or propose is clearly understood in the context of creating an agreement. If you want to test an idea, pose it using 'if'.

'What *if* we were to offer you an option to move in early – is that something that you think would add value for you as part of this agreement?'

'How about *if* we were able to leave some of the furniture for you to use in the short term? Is that something that would be useful for you?

This way you get to test the variables you think may be valuable and see whether they really will add value to the deal for the other party. There is no point in offering extra variables if the other party doesn't see how they will add value for them.

In the same way, if you'd like to ask them to consider whether they could offer certain variables of value to you, you can still use the 'if' formula.

'What *if* we asked you to delay the move by a couple of weeks; is that something you would consider?'

'*If* we were to ask you to let us use yours as a reference flat, so we could show future renters what a completed project looked like, is that something you may consider doing for us?'

Testing all your possible variables in this way, before you propose them as part of the deal, will help you to gauge what factors will add the most value, and consider how you can craft the most effective deal for all parties.

try it now TESTING VARIABLES WITH 'IF'

In the negotiation you've been preparing for in these exercises, you should now have some extra variables that might make the agreement work better for all. Think about how you may suggest the variables be part of the deal in the discussion phase. What questions can you ask using the word *if* that will test the other party's likelihood of accepting and valuing the suggestion in the final agreement? This is an important exercise, as it's critical to have some suggestions whenever you enter a discussion around an agreement. If you can, practise making suggestions using *if* until you feel comfortable with the formula.

IMPROVING YOUR CHANCES OF LISTENING WELL

In an average day we receive hundreds of emails, consume thousands of brand messages, and have many more thousands of thoughts. Our minds are therefore incredibly busy all the time and so by the time we sit down with another person to talk, we are often so full of ideas that it is hard to really listen. During many conversations we are so eager to be heard that we use the time the other person is speaking as a chance to prepare what we want to say. This is not listening, not real listening, which is critical if we are to create more creative, collaborative agreements.

try it now JUST LISTEN

Try noticing how good your listening skills really are. Notice in your next conversations how many times you are preparing to respond. Notice how much space there is between the person speaking and your response. See if you can leave time for a three-second gap between the person you are speaking to finishing their last sentence and your response. This seems simple, but it's easier said than done, and it can lead to remarkable results. You may find the other person says much more. You may also find that your mind quietens a little. Knowing you will have time to think before you respond often releases internal pressure that can otherwise lead to poor listening and premature response.

One day some years ago while travelling on a busy train in India, I was helping a local practise his English. He was mixing up the words 'listening' and 'hearing', and I was struggling to find a way of describing the difference between the two verbs. How would you describe the difference? Think about that for a moment. The critical difference is that listening is active, whereas hearing is passive. You can hear without listening, but you cannot listen without hearing. To really listen you have to engage yourself fully into the work of listening, without spending precious energy trying to work out what to say or do next.

Active listening is the act of using physical and verbal tools to support your listening. So often when we intend to listen, we are actually doing little more than hearing, and so we don't follow or understand everything that's being said. When you are really listening, your body language and verbal clues support you. You may be leaning in, tilting your head, nodding and inserting um's, yes's, or ah-ha's to help you really follow what is being said. This is why face-to-face meetings are the best place to have the kind of collaborative discussion that is critical to getting exceptional agreements; it's just easier to do all of this when you are looking into each other's eyes. How you set up this meeting will help support good listening and a collaborative discussion. A quiet space, free of distractions, and a clear and open agenda will also support you.

Alan Sharland, one of the UK's leading experts on conflict counselling and author of *How to Resolve Bullying in the Workplace*, advocates going beyond active listening to what he calls 'Co-Active Listening'. In this practice you actively repeat what has been said and ask if you have fully understood it. It is a simple, yet remarkably effective way of making sure you are listening. As the emphasis is on understanding, you put aside your response, until you are sure the other person has been understood. This kind of 'deep listening' really helps to move forward collaborative negotiations.

What often surprises me is how a little amount of listening can often go so far to building rapport and enabling you to come up with creative solutions to issues. Often our inability to stop and really listen gets in the way of understanding what is going on in a situation. Just the act of listening is all we need to allow the other party the space to tell us what the real issue is, and therefore what the solution is likely to be.

Recently I found myself in a situation that many parents will be familiar with. I had come home a little later than I expected thanks to tube delays and was looking forward to reading to my children before bed, particularly as I hadn't been at home for a few nights. I was keen to get on with the storytelling, as I was excited about the dinner to follow too. I asked my son Ziggy to brush his teeth first, and he simply refused. Being a little rushed,

I didn't really notice what was happening and repeated my request a few times until I was starting to lose my patience with him. Before raising my voice I turned to my youngest, Saffi, to ask her (albeit a little sarcastically) why she thought Ziggy didn't want to brush his teeth.

'Why don't you ask him?' she said.

'I just have asked him, and if you noticed he isn't saying anything,' I retorted.

'But you don't look like you are ready to listen,' said Saffi, 'so I imagine he's not ready to tell you yet then.'

What my six-year-old daughter had said touched a raw truth. In the rush to do it all, I had neglected to listen, so I shouldn't have been surprised that we weren't getting very far. I realized I'd have to really listen to get through this one, and that would involve putting down my phone and putting down my ideas about how and when I thought things 'should' happen.

I dropped to the bathroom floor and sat with Ziggy for a few minutes until I had a sense he was ready to speak. Something happened as I left all my thoughts behind me and prepared to really focus on what was going on in front of me. What was interesting is that as soon as my own annoyance fell away and I was ready to listen, it was clear Ziggy was ready to speak. And the answer was so far away from what I could have expected, it was remarkable. Ziggy was desperate to read to me, and he had it in his mind that once he had brushed his teeth, his time for reading would be over for good. He was so keen to read to me, and had promised his teacher he would, so he wasn't prepared to brush his teeth until he'd done it. It was a simple misunderstanding, but on reflection understandable as his Mum usually insisted on the same routine. For me, however, it showed the power of real listening in the real world to uncover things you don't really know or understand. And while we may think that uncommunicative children are worlds apart from adults in the workplace in terms of how we communicate, there are plenty of examples of customers and partners who say even less, unless they have a sense that they are really being heard.

try it now CO-ACTIVE LISTENING AT HOME OR WORK

Ask someone you know to practise Co-Active Listening with you. Choose any topic, although you may get more value if you discuss an issue over which you have had some misunderstanding in the past. The purpose of the exercise is not to seek an outcome to the issue, but to deepen your understanding, which may contribute to finding an outcome.

Using a timer set for five minutes, ask them to explain their point of view. Keep asking questions if you need to get a better understanding, but avoid saying anything yourself other than clarifying questions. Let the timer run until the end, and once they have finished do your best to summarize what they have said. Once you have repeated their point of view, ask them what you missed. Ask them if there is anything you didn't get clearly, and stay in listening mode. Repeat the exercise with you as the speaker, and notice how different it is to be listened to when the only aim of the listener is to understand. This exercise is a critical step to better listening and increased understanding.

Taking this attitude into your discussions and negotiation strategy yields results every time. If the person you are talking to feels you are really listening for understanding they will tell you more, and start to understand the benefits of collaboration for themselves.

QUESTIONING – ASKING OPEN QUESTIONS

> *I keep six honest serving-men*
> *(They taught me all I knew);*
> *Their names are What and Why and When*
> *And How and Where and Who.*
>
> Rudyard Kipling, 'The Elephant's Child'

The easiest way to create a productive discussion is to use the kind of questions that open up the other person's thinking. These questions will be ones that people can't answer with a simple 'yes' or 'no'. We call them 'open questions', and they are the foundation for creative communication. There are six words that start questions to which you can't answer 'yes' or 'no', and they are: *why, what, where, when, how* and *who*. Many of you will already know the importance of this kind of questioning because, if you are in sales, consultancy, medicine, mediation or are a counsellor, you would have been taught them as a foundation for improved communication. What amazes me though is that, despite this idea being simple, people often fail to use open questions at critical times. When we are trying to start a truly collaborative discussion using open questions, starting with one of these six words, will be critical to inspire dialogue.

Open questions, alongside good listening, create good conversations that lead to understanding, and a better chance of the creation of an agreement that really works for both parties. Something else happens too, which is almost magical: rapport develops. Robert Cialdini's research on persuasion, which he outlines in *Influence: The Psychology of Persuasion*, tells us that people are more likely to enter into an agreement with someone they like, and developing a liking for someone happens as a by-product of most genuine conversations. When you watch people in public places, you can often see rapport developing or being broken, based on the quality of the parties' ability to question and listen effectively. I remember watching a friend being 'chatted up' in a bar. After twenty minutes of intense discussion, when she returned to our table, I questioned her about the man she had been talking to. She couldn't recall his name, his occupation, where he lived or anything about him. All she could say was that he 'was really nice'. While many participants laugh when they hear this story, we all do it. My friend had been doing most of the talking, but the fact that she had been listened to, and the questions had kept flowing, were enough to build a sense of liking and rapport. This is because as humans we long to be heard, and we open up to others who are able to listen to us.

try it now ASKING OPEN QUESTIONS

Think of your negotiation. At this point, you need to discuss with the other party what your positions are and how you will collaborate. Without thinking about it too much, write down up to twenty questions that if answered will get you a better understanding of what the other party needs from the agreement and what they will be able to give to achieve that. Imagine they are with you as you conduct the exercise and that you could ask them anything you want to develop your understanding and the agreement.

Don't censor yourself if you are writing closed (yes/no) questions; just let yourself finish and then work through your questions. Notice how many questions were closed and how many were open. Rewrite the closed questions as open questions (it can always be done), but bear in mind that this is not a hard and fast rule, and sometimes you will need to ask closed questions – to determine someone's real Red Lines, for example.

SOCRATIC QUESTIONING – THE WHY BENEATH THE WHY

To have a productive discussion, it's not enough though just to ask some open questions. Real conversations don't work that way, and in reality even many open questions can easily be answered with one-word or short responses. Good conversations require the use of deeper questioning to explore the other person's ideas in such a way that is natural, builds trust and develops greater understanding. The Greek philosopher Socrates was well known for his use of exploratory questions. He proposed to let 'the answer be the mother of the next questions'. In practice, this means using words from the other person's answer to form the next (open) question. This practice can be very powerful for two reasons. It enables you not to worry about the next question until the answers have been fully given, improving your chances of real rapport and understanding. It also means that the other person gets to know that you are really listening, because they can hear some of what they have said in your response. Why it is so effective is that the other person unconsciously builds rapport with you as a result of hearing the extent of your listening. It's a valuable tool for a negotiator, and if you aren't familiar with how it works, it's really worth practising using it as much as you can. It has an almost magical way of building understanding and commitment, especially when it's used in the context of genuinely seeking mutual gain.

Here is an example of Socratic questioning as might be used by a TV interviewer:

> 'What appealed to you about this movie?'
> 'There were a lot of parallels with my own life.'
>
> 'What parallels did you see with your own life that interested you?'
> 'My father, like the character, was an alcoholic ...'
>
> 'How were you able to bring the experience of your father into your role?'

Here is an example, observed in a recent client meeting:

> 'What are you going to achieve from this project?'
> 'We are looking to break the mould of what we are doing as marketeers.'
>
> 'How are you planning to break that mould?'
> 'By providing an experience that is unexpected, exciting and transformational.'
>
> 'What support do you need to make the experience truly transformational?'

In negotiation, the use and mastery of Socratic questioning is often the make-or-break skill, as it unlocks understanding that can often produce the variables and balanced exchanges that create truly collaborative agreements. Your ability to use this technique in a way that is genuine is key. You can't just ask questions that contain snippets of a previous response, you have to get into the previous response and ask your question having understood that response, or seeking to understand that response. That foundation of real understanding is key to creating an atmosphere of agreement that promotes partnership and collaborative values.

At Microsoft they call this the 'why beneath the why'. In attempting to become what CEO Satya Nadella calls a 'customer obsessed' business, they urge everyone in the company to try to understand the deeper motivations behind customer behaviours and requests. Adopting the Socratic approach to questioning will help you to understand the 'why beneath the why' to understand *beyond* what your negotiation partner initially tells you. This will help you, and your partner, develop an increased understanding of what will work better for them in the long term in crafting an agreement with you.

try it now CONVERSATIONS AT HOME

Try to observe the art of conversation at play with your family or friends. Notice how good conversations will more often than not involve follow-up questions and deeper exploration. Notice how many questions are asked that are open, and how many are closed. Notice the difference in the responses. Notice how the level of rapport is just as vital as the type of questioning in eliciting a deeper response.

try it now CONVERSATIONS AT WORK

See if you can sit in on a meeting where someone else is having a discussion about a future agreement. You may only be able to sit beside someone while they are on the phone, but even in this position you can build your insight into the impact of questioning and listening on building understanding in negotiations. On a piece of paper, mark down how many questions were asked. Note how many were open and how many were closed. Also note how 'Socratic' they were – how well did they frame questions around the previous answers? In doing this exercise, you will start to build your understanding of how questioning and listening go hand in hand to build better relationships and agreements.

CLOSED QUESTIONS

The opposite of open questions are closed questions, those designed, intentionally or otherwise, to elicit just a 'yes' or a 'no'. These questions can often damage a relationship and rapport as they can come across as interrogational. The reason they so often fail in the discussion phase is that they are often based on assumptions, or a belief that we already know what the answer will be. In the courtroom, they are sometimes called 'leading questions', and while they may seem clever if you are trying to catch a witness out, they are not effective if you are looking to build understanding.

An example of a closed question would be: 'Is this really important to you?' It could be better phrased as: 'How important is this to you?'

'Do you have any other options?' may elicit a more open response if phrased as, 'What other options do we have?'

This isn't to say that closed questions shouldn't be used in negotiation; they remain a critical tool in the negotiation process, as they build patterns of agreement and test our partners' real responses.

Closed questions should be used throughout the discussion phase to clarify and confirm what is really important to the other person. We should be looking to get as many positive responses to our ideas as possible, partly so we build a pattern of agreement as we move throughout the negotiation. This is important if we are to get to a final agreement. While this is a technique that is used a lot by salespeople and may thus be considered a little tacky, or lacking integrity, it is vital if we are looking to create real agreement. Consistently testing our understanding and ideas is a key part of the process. Confirming regularly, in combination with asking more open questions for deeper understanding, is likely to lead to more creative variables, and more effective outcomes.

THE POWER OF PAUSE

One of the habits I picked up from my father was rummaging through second-hand bookstores, car boot sales and garage sales looking for interesting books. One such book was *The Art of Listening* by Erich Fromm, a collection of writing primarily concerned with improving psychoanalysts' ability to create impact in their clients' worlds. In the book, I discovered a simple idea about waiting for five seconds after the client has finished speaking before following up with a question or comment. I spent some time practising this in business, and, like Fromm's observation of the results it yielded in interpersonal understanding, it yielded remarkable results in commercial understanding. There is something very special about silence that enables understanding, and when you and the people around you get used to it, you'll find a huge number of things happen. The first thing is that people often reveal so much more in the silence that follows a comment than they do in the comment itself. The added depth, context and content can often in itself add layers of meaning and understanding to every conversation.

People tend to read two things into the silence, either a request for more understanding, or an appreciation of the importance of what has been said. In testing out the five-second silence in business, I found that I gained more understanding, even when nothing more was being said. It enabled me to focus on really listening to what was being said, rather than waiting my turn to speak. And I found that once people got used to the depth of conversation it inspired, it seemed natural to create that space, and genuine to want time to reflect and respond in a careful and considered way. While five seconds may seem right in a therapeutic setting, I soon began to experiment and settled on about three seconds as enough time to really feel present, and to let the person know they were being heard. It's a simple idea, but I've never heard anyone who has tried it who hasn't seen almost instant results in terms of rapport, respect and response.

try it now THE THREE-SECOND SILENCE CHALLENGE

Think of a conversation you will have today or tomorrow that is important. Can you commit to trying the three-second silence challenge? You can do this face-to-face or on the phone (although bear in mind that it will seem longer over the phone). Notice what happens when the person you are speaking to feels they are really being heard.

Try to use the silence in as many situations as you can over the next week. Notice how it affects your relationships and your understanding of others. Combine this with great questioning and listening skills to deepen your understanding.

A NOTE ON QUESTIONING SKILLS AND RAPPORT

A word of warning. Open questions don't create rapport automatically; they just help you and the person you are negotiating with get into the right zone where you are ready to ask and listen. Neil Rackham's research into this process is expanded on in his classic book on sales skills, *SPIN Selling*. In it, he suggests that open questions aren't as important as some writers may want you to believe. This is because rapport and relationship are as important as the questions you ask. Think about this: if you asked your partner the closed question, 'Did you have a nice day?' you would almost definitely get a more detailed response than if you asked a complete stranger the open variation of the question: 'How was your day?' In fact, when we have deep levels of trust and rapport, no matter what kind of questions we ask, we will get the answers we need. In negotiations, however, particularly in the discussion stage, people are often a little wary, and relationships are sometimes under pressure.

Therefore, it is important in negotiations to pay careful attention to your language and tone, as well as to the questions you ask. This will pay dividends in increasing understanding and respect. If you ask closed questions in an environment where someone feels a little under pressure, or you haven't yet built good levels of trust, then you can't expect an open response. Your attitude, though, and the extent to which you really care about making the deal a mutually beneficial arrangement will also have a positive influence on the answers you are given, as much as the questions you ask.

case study VEGINOTS – LIFE, DEATH, TERRORISTS, SECRETS AND HUMAN RESPONSES

In one of my favourite negotiation exercises, my company gives teams a complex scenario in which they are asked to play the role of research scientists. When we are really going for it, we even give them white coats to wear, which always somehow seems to make the negotiation a little more realistic and a little tenser. Both teams have separate briefs: one team are researchers creating an antidote to a rare disease that is killing children in the developing world; the other team is creating an antidote to a chemical weapon that has been developed by terrorists, which may soon be launched against major cities across the world. Both teams are told they need their ingredients from an experimental melon, the (imaginary) Veginot, which is in extremely short supply. They are told they must negotiate with the other team of scientists to receive as many Veginots as possible.

What ensues is often a full-blown discussion about the merits of their research and the likelihood and numbers of deaths projected. More often, the team working on the national security issue cloaks their project in secrecy and fails to give much away, apart from the importance and urgency of their need for the Veginot.

They often get stuck in their position and sometimes even a little confrontational. Both teams have been given big budgets and heart-rending stories of the impact if they fail to produce the antidote. The result is often conflict and/or huge bids for the Veginots and a failure to collaborate to use them in any way.

They are also given one piece of information that they rarely pick up on. One team needs the seeds and the other team needs the rind from this fruit. It is remarkable how few teams (without prompting) ask enough questions of the other team to really understand not just what they're doing, but why and how they're doing it. As soon as the teams start to ask why and how, a mutually agreeable solution occurs. The exercise points us to a simple truth: if you don't know the why, how, where, when and who, then the what can sometimes be irrelevant. Genuine curiosity has to be the guiding principle of the discussion phase as you seek first to understand, then to be understood.

GETTING AGREEMENT AND BUILDING A COLLABORATIVE ATTITUDE

So, we've talked about rapport in relation to asking open questions and in relation to showing the right attitude, but how do we really bring those together? The secret to creating rapport is in the authenticity of the listening. For so many years, I believed that it was the kind of questions you asked that produced the rapport. What I now understand, however, is the questions only create the space. Rapport is just what happens when you allow your thinking to get out of the way, and you engage genuinely with another human being. Author, leadership speaker and coach Chantal Burns helped me understand this, and her book *Instant Motivation* points to a simple idea which shows us that our thinking is the key barrier to connections with others. When we allow our internal monologue to be put largely to one side, we create genuine connection, increased rapport and deeper understanding. We will explore this in more detail in Chapter 9, Understanding the Human Operating System, where we will see how our listening is affected by our internal monologue, and by a misunderstanding of how our feelings are created. For now, it's worth noting that listening is an essential skill for crafting agreements that give more to each party. Without great listening, assumptions abound and disappointment, conflict and mismatched expectations are sure to follow.

case study

KATHLEEN'S STORY: ESTABLISHING DIALOGUE

Kathleen knows that ultimately the HR Director and CEO are going to put together a package to propose to her, but she wants to influence the process as much as possible and so enters her discussion with the HR Director with a very open agenda. She focuses on her enthusiasm about the role and asks to discuss potential scenarios, even though she is aware the decision between herself and the other candidate has not been made.

Importantly, she says very little and listens carefully to the HR Director, hearing about the pressure he is under managing recruitment and retention in sites across the globe. Through this, she also discovers different approaches to working that newly acquired offices in Scandinavia have brought to the group. Having listened, she learns that the decision needs time, partly because of the people involved, and partly because there is a new acquisition she hadn't known about in the Far East that is taking up the board's time.

The discussion didn't occur in just one meeting, and she was able to continue with it at an SLT (Senior Leadership Team) Summit with the CEO later in the month. What was clear though is that her discussion with the HR Director and the CEO gave the opportunity to suggest ideas and present possible solutions to problems she hadn't known existed. The HR Director shared her issues with creating a people development programme for the business, and the CEO shared concerns about how the HR Director was coping. When the final proposal involved her taking control of a certain aspect of the HR role for Europe – the people development side she had championed early in her career – she could see that having an open dialogue about her expectations, and listening to her colleagues, had created opportunities for all the parties that may not have existed before.

You may not (at this stage at least!) be negotiating a six-figure salary and a place on the board, but no matter the scale or stakes in your negotiation, can you see how investing time in more open dialogue is beneficial before you move on to creating a proposal?

case study SIMON'S STORY: WORKING AROUND BARRIERS TO DISCUSSION

Simon is struggling to get access to Luca, his bank contact, to have a meaningful dialogue about what they want. The bank is demanding a proposal immediately and even though they had said that Simon's company won the 'pitch', the bank is now intimating that other agencies are still in the frame, particularly if they don't reach an agreement on fees shortly.

As a result, Simon has to get something across to them, so he drafts what he calls a 'Preliminary Proposal'. In it he mentions a range for the hourly rate and a number of other factors. He requests a meeting to discuss the proposal and fortunately manages to extend it to include lunch. By the end of the lunch he feels that he really has a better idea of what is needed. He has started to get an understanding of 'the why beneath the why'. He has learned more about Luca, his motivations and what he wants from the whole project, and not just from the deal.

In fact, he realizes that the contract itself is far from Luca's mind, just a task on a to-do list to pass on to procurement. The digital element of the work is what excites him, and is relatively new to the bank. It was what had won them the work, and what Luca was banking on (excuse the pun) for his and the project's success.

This discussion enables Simon to frame a final (well almost final) agreement that Luca is happy to pass through to procurement for final negotiations. Fortunately, what Luca had explained in the discussion also reveals the procurement team's relative inexperience in the digital field. Thus Simon is able to produce a proposal that really meets the marketing and the procurement teams' needs. Offering a solid rate that the bank is able to cross-reference with other agency rates, and having more flexibility on the digital delivery, works well for everyone, especially as Simon outsources much of the digital work to a set of contractors in Bulgaria that offer exceptional value to him.

What can you learn about the value of discussion from applying Simon's lessons to your situation? How can you postpone making a formal proposal until you have had a good discussion and discovered more about 'the why beneath the why' for the person or business you are negotiating with?

CHECKLIST FOR DISCUSSION PHASE

1. Have you shared your intention for being collaborative with the other party?

2. Does the other party understand what collaborative negotiation is about, and have they bought into the concept?

3. Are you clear about the power of using 'if' as a tool for conditionality?

4. Have you set up a time and place for this discussion that will minimize distractions?

5. What can you do to maximize the chances that you will be able to listen empathetically?

6. Have you identified some questions you can ask that will deepen your understanding of the why beneath the why?

7. Are you ready to suspend judgement and ask Socratic questions to deepen your understanding of their needs?

CHAPTER 6

Step Five – Proposing

Getting a proposal on to the table is a critical part of getting to agreement. Someone needs to do it first, and many experts have different views on the merits of laying your cards on the table. I remember a classic interview with the Palestinian Leader Yasser Arafat, when he was being pushed by veteran BBC political host Sir Robin Day on whether the Palestine Liberation Organization would accept Israel's right to exist as a precursor to direct negotiations with the Israeli government. Arafat referred to a game of cards, and suggested that showing one's hand before the cards have been turned is a bad strategy. He implied that he had the card (recognition of Israel) in his hand but refused to be pushed on when he would play it. He died without having ever played it. His successor was willing to play it, and even though it did little to end the conflict, it did get the parties to the same table for a while in Oslo.

Your negotiations are not games of cards, nor was the future of the Palestinians. Playing games around negotiations will prolong them, decrease rapport and lead to a win–lose mindset that causes unnecessary delay, stagnation and suffering. If the object of the game is for both parties to win, the more open you can be with your hand, the more likely you will be to get an agreement that works for all. That doesn't mean being naive. If you can see in your preparation that your partner is unwilling to cooperate, then you may need to manoeuvre a little to find an outcome that works for both of you. If you have seen a competitive streak in your partner, then you may have to accept that only by letting them feel they have won will you be able to genuinely carve an agreement that works for both of you. If you have realized that it is you who has the competitive streak, then you may need to adjust your expectations now in planning your proposal.

You should be working towards creating a proposal that you can put forward with confidence that it will be accepted at the first go. If you have done your research well enough, that will often be the case, but we don't always live in an ideal world, so you need to be prepared for some bargaining. For this reason, you always need to build into your proposal some room for trading around key variables. According to your reading of your negotiation partner and the situation, you should design the proposal so that it can either be accepted as is, or so that both parties have room to move and still create a mutually acceptable agreement.

The important thing to remember is that all you are creating here is a 'proposal' for agreement, not a final deal. Knowing that this is a proposal that will go through a stage of bargaining will enable you to include a level of flexibility in your approach. Looking at your Green Zone of Agreement, you should be able to pick a list of variables that can be exchanged by both parties to come to a sound agreement. You won't want to include all the variables you have on your or your partner's lists; making it simple and clear is critical at this stage. Choose the most important variables that are on your list and the ones that you think you partner values most. You must make your proposal conditional, by using the magic word 'if'. Remember that in all agreements there should be conditions that are met by both parties, so make sure you aren't one-sided in your approach by just listing what you are prepared to offer.

It is also important not to put too much into a first proposal. You should be looking to make it easy to accept, even if that means leaving out variables that you will want to include as you finalize the agreement. Any potentially costly or volatile clauses or variables should be written specifically in the proposal, but you may not need to list every variable at this stage.

THE POWER OF THE WRITTEN WORD

The written word is often a more powerful medium than conversation, but given its more concrete nature, you should use it only when you are confident that your proposal is sound, and is close enough to be accepted as is. If you have had an honest and effective discussion, this should be possible, so an email or note will work well to move the negotiation forward. In many cases you will need to formalize the process in this way. Often a call will be the best way to make the initial proposal though, because it will allow you to gauge the reaction and determine whether to move directly on to the bargaining and agreement stage. There are no hard-and-fast rules though for how to present a proposal. What is important is that you recognize that, following a clear discussion, one party will need to proactively present a proposal. And if you are the person doing that, then you are more likely to be able to move the agreement in a direction that works well for both parties.

The advantage of being the person who puts forward the first proposal is that you stay in the driving seat. As long as you don't propose anything that is clearly unaligned with your discussions, then you should be able to use the proposal as a step to moving the agreement on. When you write your proposal, allow yourself room to move in the next stage, Bargaining (which we will cover in the next chapter). This means you will need to write your proposal using variables that both you and your partner may be able to exchange, or bargain with, to move the agreement forward.

STATING THE BENEFITS – THE 'WHY' BENEATH THE 'HOW'

Sometimes, once we get into the logistics of our negotiations in a project, we can lose focus of why we are negotiating in the first place. A neighbour may be negotiating about some aspect of their fence so they can enjoy their garden; an employee may be negotiating over a contract of employment so they can carry on serving the firm's clients; an advertiser may be negotiating a TV deal so they can promote their products on a specific platform. Don't forget to mention this at the heart of your proposal. The 'how' is clearly the focus of any proposal, but a reference to this reason, the 'why', will set the framework for a positive collaboration. What that means is that we should be clear in our own minds not just what the deal will give the other party, but why it is important to them. Stating this in our proposal is important. It reminds the other party of the important reasons beneath the technical, day-to-day workings of the deal.

We should remember that the proposal stage, particularly when the negotiation is happening in a remote setting, is where delays and inaction can thwart progress and kill deals. Many an enthusiastic negotiator has had the wind taken out of their sails through the process of getting to 'yes', and enthusiasm can easily wane. All parties need to stay motivated, especially if a lot is at stake, or if an alternative may be found, like doing a deal with someone else, or not doing a deal at all. It's therefore critical to understand what is really motivating the other party and make sure you remind them of these driving factors at the time they are considering your offer. We can do this by connecting our partner's motivations with active language that shows how the deal responds to their motivations and fulfils their needs.

Abraham Maslow, the acclaimed American psychologist, posited that all human behaviour is predicated on unfulfilled needs. His famous Hierarchy of Needs model suggests that human behaviour can be understood if we look at which unfulfilled need may be driving a person's thoughts or behaviour. His theory was that all human behaviour is 'activated' by an unfulfilled need, and that humans have a hierarchy of needs, which ranges from our most basic Physiological needs (like food and drink), through needs based on Security, our Social role, Self-Esteem and finally the need for Self-Actualization.

If we had no unfulfilled needs, we would literally never get out of bed. Being clear what our, and our partner's, unfulfilled needs are that might be met through the deal will help us to create a proposal that motivates action and provokes a response. When we have understood those needs in the preparation and discussion phases, we will be able to connect this in our proposals in a way that reminds them of those needs, and suggests a way to fulfil them.

MAKING A CALL TO ACTION

A good proposal will enable the person reading it to make a decision, and will have an intention agreement – a call to action, or a simple statement that helps the receiver push the button on completing the deal. The intention agreement may be a simple note in an email that asks the receiver to reply with their comments directly, or a request for a follow-up meeting. It may even be a click-through mechanism that allows the other person to accept the offer immediately. Whether it is a suggested date for a meeting to agree, or a request for a follow-up call, it should be clear in your proposal what the next steps are, and the easiest way for the other person to take them.

Adding to your proposals the essential terms and conditions that you would anticipate in any final agreement is a good way to accelerate deals. If you intend to create a formal contract, then referencing that at this stage will help you set expectations and clarify timelines. Personally, I often place my key terms at the bottom of my email proposals, as I tend to create proposals and agreements through this more informal channel, rather than turning the proposal into a legal contract. That way I can ask my clients simply to return the email that I used to send the proposal with any suggested changes, and I'm happy that this is all the documentation I need. The important thing for you is to state in your proposal any intentions you have about contracts, so that it can be factored into your partner's response.

case study

KATHLEEN'S STORY: RESPONDING TO AN OFFER

Eventually Kathleen is called to LA to have the final 'interview' for her role, but she knows on the plane that she is going to be offered the job, as she has never been booked on First Class before – a privilege she knows is reserved for the board.

In the interview, when she has the proposal in her hand, it feels like a fait accompli, but Kathleen asks for time to reflect. She uses a third party (consulting with her husband) and a particular clause (lines of reporting) as her reason for this request and is given time. In doing so, she is able to make a counterproposal that tweaks the proposal a little: rearranging reporting structures. Knowing that any proposal is reasonably followed by bargaining, she gives herself time to think and to include some additional variables, in a way that makes more sense to her and, ultimately, improves the business.

case study

SIMON'S STORY: REWORKING A PROPOSAL

While Luca accepts Simon's proposal, the subsequent rejection by the procurement team was well anticipated because Simon understands the pressure they face to create savings. Because of this understanding, Simon has allowed himself flexibility and, although the process isn't easy, he finally creates a proposal after a few attempts that was able to move them forward.

Make sure that your proposals are clear enough, and yet contain enough flexibility to create a deal moving forward.

CHECKLIST FOR EFFECTIVE PROPOSALS

1. Have you demonstrated and articulated the benefit of the key elements of the proposal? Have you shown how the proposal meets the unfulfilled needs of your partner?

2. Is your proposal positioned high enough above both parties' Red Lines to enable bargaining for agreement?

3. Does your proposal contain effective variables that contain high value to both parties?

4. Does your written proposal contain a call to action that will enable the other party to accept your proposal?

5. Have you added references to any additional legal terms and conditions you intend to apply?

6. Have you referenced the need to create a binding legal contract if that is your intention at the end of the negotiation?

CHAPTER 7

Step Six – Bargaining

The most important lesson you can ever learn about bargaining is to use the phrase: 'If you ..., then I ...' This simple phrase gets to the heart of what negotiation really is, the art of getting agreement. It demonstrates the balanced nature of negotiations and the mutual exchange required to get agreement. Its structure also ensures that you remain equal, and that the other party understands the nature of the exchange you are proposing. Putting 'If you' at the start of the phrase adds conditionality to every statement you make, and ensures the other person understands that what follows would only be given dependent on an exchange. Remember the lesson that Millie taught me, when I reversed the phrase (If I ..., then you ...) and she demanded two cookies for two shoes? Reversing the phrasing really can make a big difference in reducing the emphasis on conditionality. Listen to it yourself. Saying 'If I give you a cookie ...' instantly overshadows what goes after it, but saying 'If you clear up the hall, then I will give you a cookie' is much more likely to get the desired response.

This golden phrase in bargaining doesn't just apply to children. When discussing a project with a client recently, when we got to fixing dates for a conference I discovered that the planned date was in the middle of my holiday. I assumed that the client would understand that extra expenses would be incurred to attend during my holiday. So I didn't say what I should have: 'If you are happy to pay the expenses involved in me coming from my holiday, then I will speak at the conference in person.' I didn't clarify this aspect, and as a result it took me eight months to get them to pay the expenses! When you are getting close to final agreement, you need to be clear what the factors are and what you are expecting. Using the phrase 'If you ..., then I ...' keeps expectations clear and avoids misunderstanding.

THE MAGIC OF *IF*

In my more overexcited moments I've suggested that the word 'if' has a magical quality in negotiations. If you think about it carefully, you may agree. 'If' contains the essence of conditionality. When you use it, you demonstrate the flexible nature of the discussion, and you highlight the conditional quality of what you are proposing. In my experience, the more 'if's I hear during negotiation role-plays, the more likely the parties are to be working collaboratively towards an agreement that works for all. Whether in preparation, discussion, proposition or during the bargaining, 'if' is a steady tool to achieve your collaborative goals.

GETTING AGREEMENT TO BARGAIN

At the heart of any negotiation is the willingness of both parties to trade what they have in order to reach agreement. All five steps so far have led towards this, but it's important to add that if one party needs to reach agreement more than the other party, then the bargaining is going to be uneven. This is why feeling like you are on an equal footing is the foundation of good bargaining. While it may not always seem to be the case, as you may be negotiating with someone who appears to have more power than you, it is an important mental step to being able to bargain effectively with another person. If the other party feels, or acts, like they have a stronger position, they will have to concede less to get a deal. Equality of bargaining power does not mean you need to be on equal terms in respect of resources, position or status, it just means that you need to accept that both parties want to reach an agreement and are interested in doing so. For this reason, just as you set out an intention agreement in your proposal in step five, it's good to state this desire at the beginning of any bargaining, and again at any point where it looks like you may be coming to an impasse. Simple questions like, 'Are we both agreed that we want to resolve this?' or 'I know we both want to make this work, don't we?' will help you both to keep equality in mind. Note the question at the end of the second example; this shows the other person that you are equal in your desire to make an agreement and then checks that they feel the same way. This agreement question is something you can return to as many times as you need to ensure you don't get into conflict or confrontation as you work out the exact nature of an agreement.

try it now CREATING AN AGREEMENT QUESTION

Write out an agreement question for your negotiation. What can you ask that will get the other person to agree that you do actually have a mutual interest in reaching an agreement? Repeat this question in a number of different negotiations you are involved in, changing the style as needed to suit the parties involved. This statement is a critical tool in bargaining. You will return to it whenever you need to.

ACTIVE LISTENING AND USING SILENCE TO GET AGREEMENT

I met a businessman in a hotel bar in Dubai who told me a fantastic story about the time he had made a proposal to a local sheikh and then waited in silence for over twenty minutes for his response. His experience and training had told him that the first person to speak after a proposal was made would be the 'loser', and so he was determined to wait for his potential customer to speak first. It's a lot longer than the three seconds I would propose, and although it comes from a mindset of winners and losers, and I suspect it was a heavily embellished bar tale, it illustrates something that successful salespeople have known for years. Silence will often help seal agreement much more readily than saying something else.

Giving the other person time to process your proposal not only demonstrates your confidence that agreement is the logical next step, it also allows them the chance to process that agreement for themselves. So, remember that if you are looking for agreement, let the other party talk. Practise using the three-second pause that we discussed in Chapter 5 to prompt agreement and acceptance of the terms.

MOVE SLOWLY AND IN SMALL STEPS

The more variables you have on your Shopping List, the easier it will be to bargain. Ideally, you should be discussing one point at a time and doing your best to take small steps. Rule out any attempt by the other party to bundle together items that are high cost to you in exchange for single concessions. In the same way, trying to exchange items of high value with items of relatively low value may also lead to impasse. Move one step at a time, making sure you use 'If you ..., then I ...' to seal agreement on each point.

It's always tempting to jump straight to a final agreement, especially when time isn't on your side, but avoid the temptation, especially if doing so means making concessions that won't make the deal better for both parties. Early in my sales career selling office equipment I was negotiating with a bright lawyer over a high-volume photocopier for his business. The deal had been going back and forth for a while, and I was keen to gain agreement (and my quarterly target) by the end of the week. When I dropped by his office on the Strand, he presented me with what I now know is a simple tactic, nicknamed the 'Columbo' (after the American TV detective whose speciality was solving the crime at the end of each show using the line, 'Just one more thing …'). We'll look at this tactic in more detail in Chapter 12. Once we had agreed what had been the sticking point earlier in the week, the service charges, I was ready to leave and generate the order that would put my monthly and quarterly commission in the bag.

'Just one more thing,' said the lawyer. 'I do want the stapler after all, and I expect you to deliver it next week while I am away, so it can be ready for me when I get back on Friday.' And with that he bundled me out of the door saying that he didn't expect to pay anything extra for the stapler on the lease as it was only a £400 extra and the total lease cost was over £6,000, so he felt we could cover that easily within the cost. The truth is I was young, a little naive, and a little desperate. Instead of asking to discuss each request one at a time, I capitulated and said nothing. Being so eager to complete the bargaining, I avoided taking it step by step and left myself with multiple hassles, a short delivery and a client who was out of town and expecting delivery without a signed contract.

What I should have done was taken each new piece of information separately and discussed them one by one: him going away, the delivery time, the stapler, the monthly cost, even the consumable costs – as we had just agreed a per-copy cost that now was going to include staples. It wasn't until the next week that I discovered how much I had given away in such a small moment. On the Monday with the client in Marbella, a stapler unit on the slow boat from China, and a service department in arms about a third-floor delivery with no lift, I realized this wasn't win–win at all. In fact, as it turned out, it wasn't even win–lose, it was kind of lose–lose, but that didn't become clear for another year. It turned out that in 1989 Canon hadn't really mastered how to make a stapler fit on a high-volume copier, so the unit malfunctioned regularly until the engineer took it off. When the lawyer's office manager called me in to complain, she told me that she had never wanted the stapler in the first place, and neither had her boss, but he had felt delighted when I had given it to him, as he felt like he had got something for nothing. Now he was trying to negotiate a reduction of his monthly charge to compensate for the lack of stapler unit on the machine. I can't tell you how it ended up because that was one of the last photocopier calls I ever made. I was so annoyed about his book *Give and Take: Why Helping Others Drives Our Success* points to an increasing body of evidence which suggests that this approach can produce better results for all. He demonstrates how the reasoning behind doing so goes beyond moral reasoning, or because it feels good. Instead, collaboration is a critical tool in a society that now relies more on networks and communities to produce results. People who understand this are creating equity that will help them and those around them to connect and produce in the future.

THE CLOCK IS TICKING – AVOIDING THE PRESSURE OF DEADLINES

One of the things that always moves negotiations forward is the pressure of time. So much so that one Japanese property investor used to leave his chauffeur outside and claim to be on the 9pm flight to Tokyo when entering critical negotiations. Once the deal had been made under pressure of time, he'd invite the other party out to dinner, even though they were expecting him to rush off for his flight! Think of the critical negotiations you hear on the news, whether it be hostage situations or peace deals; deadlines will be seen to add pressure and stimulate response. Be careful that in bargaining you are not seduced by the pressure of time. You need to allow enough time to think, plan and discuss with others if need be. Time pressure can often cause you to make decisions you may not have made otherwise, which may cause long-term regret and deals that aren't really in everyone's best interests.

TAKING TIME-OUTS

While you are bargaining, you should be prepared to take 'time-outs' whenever you feel you need to. These breaks will allow both parties to think clearly and creatively. If you are planning a challenging negotiation, it's a good idea to plan a few breaks, so you have space to consider the options. Decisions made with perspective produce more lasting agreement and less doubt and resentment. This applies at any time during any negotiation. Don't allow yourself to be pushed into making an agreement too quickly. Often you may be able to use another party – such as a colleague or supplier – as a reason to add breaks, so you can liaise and confirm items that need to be in the agreement. In the world of advertising sales, we would often gain a little perspective when negotiating with advertising agencies by asking for time to speak to our scheduling departments about specifics of the deals we were planning. By including these breaks, we were able to sit down with others and discuss our positions to make sure we were building deals that would work well in the short and long term. Often when you are pushed into making deals quickly, you miss out on adding variables that could benefit both you and the other party.

try it now TAKING A TIME-OUT

Thinking about negotiations that you have in the pipeline, how can you work in time-outs to ensure you have enough time to think clearly and consider all the perspectives? Who can you use as a sounding board to run over the terms of the deal and get ideas for how you may be able to work towards better terms for all? How might you be able to position these time-outs with your negotiation partner so they can see the value too?

Do bear in mind, however, that the longer you leave a deal open, the more chances you give the other party to find an alternative to doing the right deal with you. Clearly you should spend a good amount of time understanding their needs and crafting a package that meets everybody's needs, but at the final stage of the negotiation it is important to be assertive and get the deal done. Don't allow your preparation and desire to negotiate effectively to become a tool for procrastination, or to unnecessarily delay agreement.

WATCH FOR INFLATION/DEFLATION

A classic negotiation tactic at this stage is to 'inflate/deflate'. This means a seasoned negotiator will try to inflate the importance of variables they are conceding while simultaneously 'deflating' the value of items they are trying to persuade you to add to the deal. If you have had a clear discussion phase, you should have a good understanding of the value of the variables you are discussing. Avoid being affected by this tactic; where it is being overplayed you can always call their bluff by pulling off the table items they are inflating or deflating. Keep it real by returning to your agreement questions, focusing on an attitude of agreement, and asking which options do have value for them.

KEEPING IN THE ZONE OF AGREEMENT

It's important in the discussion phase to remain positive and collaborative and to ensure that you are not talked out of your Green Zone, and into a place that you will subsequently regret. Make certain that you are not moving below any of your Red Lines, and that, if they are mentioned, you are clear that you are not moving on those points. What is interesting, however, is that when you get into a truly collaborative mode, you may notice that your Red Lines begin to blur a little. That's because in some circumstances you will be prepared to move on what seem like clear boundaries, if the other party is prepared to do something extraordinary. Remember that extraordinary results are possible when you work in extraordinary ways, so be open to anything, while keeping your boundaries clear. If your boundaries have begun to blur, go back to your preparation work from step two, and reassess your Win Matrix, paying particular attention to those bottom and Red Lines.

That said, you need to let the other party know that you are prepared to not do the deal if the conditions are not right. Stating this clearly will make it easier for all parties to focus on being truly collaborative. This is not a question of playing hardball, but a matter of being clear and fair. You should be confident enough that you can add value both ways, but clear enough that if the conditions don't work for both of you it doesn't need to damage your personal or professional relationships. I understand that in many cases this will seem impossible, especially when we are dealing with long-term business or professional relationships, but it doesn't need to be the case that if you don't do a deal, your relationship needs to suffer.

case study
WALKING AWAY AND MAINTAINING RELATIONSHIPS

I had a difficult conversation a few years ago with a client that had just been through a takeover. I was very emotionally involved, having worked for the original business myself years before, and having worked with them subsequently for many years as a consultant. I was close to many people there, and they represented a good part of my income. They were planning a lot of training, and we had some great ideas about what was next for their staff. They wanted to consolidate suppliers and wanted me to quote for much more work, so there was a lot on the table for us all.

During our discussion phase, however, the assumptions I had made in my preparations were challenged. There were lots of suppliers willing to undercut my business by around 50 per cent, and even with the large volume under discussion, I couldn't see how we would be able to find genuine agreement. I had business partners with whom I needed to discuss my instinct, which was to turn down this large contract. So I asked for time to discuss it with my partners, which was a genuine need.

However, I do regret that I wasn't more honest at that meeting about the likelihood of doing a deal, as it wasted both of our time having another meeting to simply agree not to agree, because our expectations on price were so far apart. That said, I am pleased we were able to discuss why I had to walk away from the discussion and why I was not going to provide a proposal at that time. Having follow-up conversations with some other key players in the business was also important, because I knew then that not only would their policy change in time, but also that our relationships would be far stronger and my company's reputation far greater because of my principled position that year. It was five years until I worked with the business again, but my relationship with key players was strengthened, not damaged, by the understanding that in the short term it wouldn't have worked for all of us for me to work with them. Years later, I'm back on their roster, working with senior team with rates and conditions that work for all of us.

case study KATHLEEN'S STORY: MAKING A TRADE

Kathleen's final bargaining creates a direct trade-off in the area of reporting. Her offer is: 'If you allow the Global Team to report through me, then I am prepared to accept that the new acquisitions will report directly to the CEO for the next 24 months'. In bargaining after receiving the initial proposal, she manages to get more control than she had initially anticipated, in exchange for something she didn't really want to have to deal with in her first two years on the board.

case study SIMON'S STORY: BARGAINING IN A TEAM

Simon enjoys the process of bargaining with procurement. Because the Procurement Manager has an assistant, Simon brings his wife, the Creative Director of the company, to the second meeting, and they work as a team. Once both sides establish that they have common goals, they trade some key variables: Simon gets movement on payment terms, in return for monthly forecasting of predicted budgets. The bank moves from their standard 60-day payment terms to a staggered approach based on payment levels; this doesn't take too much effort on the bank's part but really helps Simon's cash flow. In return, it's not a high cost for Simon's team to provide more visibility for the bank about upcoming fees, but it really helps the bank to manage their spending. This is what makes it a genuinely mutually beneficial exchange.

What will you be prepared to trade to bring your agreements to a mutually satisfying outcome?

CHECKLIST FOR BARGAINING

1. Are you clear about your Red Lines, and is the other party clear about them?

2. Are you comfortable walking away; do you have an alternative?

3. Are you comfortable telling the other party that you will walk away if you don't reach an agreement?

4. Are you prepared and ready to call a time-out so you can review your position or get some advice?

5. Are you clear which variables you are going to bargain with?

6. Can you see how you can use 'If you ..., then I ...' to seal agreement on key points?

7. What are the timelines for this negotiation, and how can you use this to reach agreement?

8. Are you still in a collaborative mindset? Is the other party?

9. What can you do to improve the chances of the other person being collaborative?

CHAPTER 8

Step Seven – Agreeing

Agreement isn't only a *stage* in your negotiations, as I trust you have seen by now, it's also an *attitude*. You will succeed in collaborative negotiations when you seek agreement from the beginning of the process – with your agreement intention and questions – right through to the end. You will get to an agreement if, throughout the process, you have been as focused on the other person's needs as on your own, and you have been prepared to look creatively at what you have all got to give to the agreement to craft something that works. Yet civil courts across the world are full of people arguing about contracts that were agreed, at least in principle. How to stop your agreement falling into such a disagreement is the subject of this chapter. You will see this is a short chapter, as this formal stage of a negotiation is the natural conclusion. If you negotiate effectively and collaboratively, agreement will happen naturally; all you need to do is make sure this agreement is stated clearly and recorded in a way that works for the situation you are in.

Good agreements are crafted in such a way that they are clear, and easy to execute. They are communicated in a way that is easy for both parties to refer to, and they are sealed in a way that makes every party to them aware of their commitments. In business this usually means they are written and drafted in such a way that they can be executed in a court of law. Yet in reality most of the agreements you will be drafting will never want to go that way, and so how you draft them will depend on which people will make them happen if all else fails. Sending an email may seem to you to be the best way to ensure someone gets something, but in reality this often means that it isn't read. If your intention is to get genuine agreement, then placing it into someone's email chain may have the opposite effect; you may delay their agreement and add levels of confusion. Ideally your agreements will be simple enough that everyone can remember them. If you are summarizing and emailing, challenge yourself to write a short enough summary that it can be read without needing to scroll down.

AGREEMENT IN ACTION

At the end of my negotiation course we run a small exercise that helps people to consolidate their learning and have a bit of fun putting the ideas into practice. In pairs participants negotiate to buy and sell some household items. Participants have fun bargaining with creative variables, and creating exchanges that add as much value as possible. Often they have crafted quite elaborate agreements in the ten minutes they are given. When everyone is done I ask them to write down what they have agreed without further discussion. Interestingly, so often what is written down by each party varies considerably. Stuff is added, forgotten or taken away. What is clear is that even moments after making an agreement, people's interpretations of it can start to get muddled, so committing the agreement to paper in some form is an important step.

Once you have decided the best medium for your agreement, you should think of a way that you can 'seal the deal'. This phrase originally comes from the Roman practice of using wax seals to countersign contracts, and the process of endorsing your agreement is worth considering. The more public you can make the agreement, the more pressure you may be able to put on both parties to keep the agreement without resorting to legal resolution. In Jewish tradition, marriage is a contractual agreement, made between a husband and wife, but the custom of marriage ceremonies has overshadowed the contract itself, as the public act has more significance to many than the legal contract. In our home we have our Marriage Contract clearly displayed in our hall. It is quite intentional. It is a piece of art that declares our intentions, to us and to visitors to our home, in a public way that helps to reinforce the commitment.

If your agreement is a private one, then you may want to commit it to paper, and have the agreement countersigned by someone that both parties respect, even if you are not going to the extent of legally drafting it. This can add moral weight to the burden of execution. You may have seen agreements on people's kitchen walls or fridges, between families or friends. All of these are valid ways to ensure there is a public declaration of the intentions and elements of your agreement.

To make an agreement legally binding there needs to be both offer and acceptance; there needs to be an exchange. Actually the law isn't as idealistic as we are, so it doesn't need to be a mutually acceptable exchange, but there does need to be an exchange. This is worth bearing in mind when crafting any written agreement. The obligations of both sides should be stated clearly, and it should be clear also what the remedies are. This means you should state what happens if the agreement is not met. In many legal documents this just means referring to the courts for remedy, but in your agreements you should make this clear if you can. (Within reason, as sometimes it will be blindingly obvious what the remedy is.)

GETTING AGREEMENT BY USING THE SET ASIDE

One tactic that often will give you time if you are getting stuck on a particular issue is the 'set aside'. What this involves is that you ask for any contentious issue which seems insolvable to be put aside, and you focus on what you can agree on. The idea is that if you can reach agreement on as many issues as possible, you may be able to return to the more difficult issue with a new perspective.

This was used very effectively in the Northern Ireland peace negotiations, which took place throughout the 1990s. As both parties found it very hard to agree on what would happen with the stockpiles of arms that had been built up during the conflict, the issue of disarmament was put aside for a long time. The peace treaty, the Good Friday Agreement, was pretty much signed and sealed, and a process for local government established before the issue was brought back to the table to be dealt with. What often happens when this tactic is used is that seemingly 'unsolvable' issues become less challenging when put beside the benefits of the agreement that has been reached. Thus in Northern Ireland once peace had been established and political power was being shared among the parties, it seemed easier to find a way to decommission the arms that might potentially threaten future peace.

DO I NEED A LAWYER TO DRAFT MY CONTRACT?

If you do want to structure your agreement in such a way that it is legally binding then the reality is that you may need to have a lawyer help you with its drafting.

Unless you are creating an agreement that is standard in many other ways, like a tenancy agreement, you will need to understand the elements of the legal process that may be used to enforce it in order to draft it correctly. This means that if you are doing business in a foreign country you will need to get a local lawyer involved. If you are dealing with a person in a different country then it may seem easier to write into the contract that it is binding by the laws of the country you are in, but if you can't extradite the person to attend court in your country it will be unenforceable anyway. That said, many contracts under dispute in the courts are well drafted. It's not only poor drafting that causes disputes, but people, and misunderstanding.

case study

KATHLEEN AND SIMON'S STORIES: FINDING AGREEMENT

Both Kathleen and Simon are in situations where a formal contract is needed: a contract of employment for Kathleen, and a statement of work and contract terms for Simon. Both need legal oversight to complete the paperwork.

Yet in reality, many contracts exist without formal written contracts. Phone calls, emails, written notes and handshakes are often all that's needed to start work on a professional or personal agreement. How can you draft something less formal that states the agreement clearly, and allows the other party an opportunity to review what you have discussed and agree to it?

CHECKLIST FOR YOUR AGREEMENTS

1. Have you agreed the terms of your agreement and written them in a form that both agree on?

2. Are both sides' commitments stated clearly (offer and acceptance)?

3. Have you agreed where you will keep the agreement and who will be the arbiter if you disagree in the future?

4. Have you shared the agreement with someone who can check it for clarity and legal enforceability (if that's what you decide is appropriate)?

5. Would a public statement support you or the other party to keep the agreement?

CHAPTER 9

Understanding the Human Operating System

You are only ever one thought away
from a completely different view
of your reality right now.

Aaron Turner, founder
of One Thought

I think, therefore I am.

René Descartes

One factor that plays a role in every negotiation, but is often overlooked by some of the most skilled business professionals, is the impact of either party's state of mind during negotiations. While this is an area that many sports professionals and coaches recognize as the 'missing link' between poor and great performance, many negotiators ignore its impact on preparation and results. In this chapter, I will share what I have learned is critical to being able to successfully craft agreements: a simple concept that when understood will bring a breakthrough in your creativity and your ability to connect with others. While this idea is simple to explain, it can be harder to grasp its role in our day-to-day interactions, and when we fail to do so, we waste time and energy. I call this important idea 'the human operating system'; it is at play in every stage of your negotiations. It works exactly the same for every person, regardless of the personality or behaviour that we have adopted. For negotiators, understanding this system – which creates our thoughts, experiences and feelings – improves our performance. It enables us to connect with our negotiation partners without the noise of anxiety and doubt that can get in the way of any personal performance, whether in a sporting, personal or professional field.

> *We see the world not as it is, but as we are.*
> Stephen Covey

The misunderstanding that plagues so many interactions is the belief that our feelings come from our circumstances, that what we are feeling is the result of the situation we find ourselves in. While it looks like this is the case, it really isn't. What I am suggesting is that we often fail to recognize that our thinking is no more than a personal point of view, created internally, and completely governed by our moods or level of awareness at a particular time. This leads to countless arguments, fruitless discussions and frustrating hours of negotiations.

Our awareness and perception of the world around us is so instinctive that we often take it for granted or mistakenly believe that this perception of the world is simply *our* reality. The feelings and emotions that we then experience, we therefore often interpret as a product of the external world.

For instance, when we see our children playing with their food, colleagues taking breaks, or our negotiation partners positioning variables in a certain way, we experience thoughts and corresponding feelings. And so we rationalize that the circumstances are *causing* the feelings. Assuming that circumstances are causing our feelings, we reason that we should attempt to change our feelings by changing our circumstances. Getting caught in this reasoning trap is completely normal and understandable, but it is counterproductive, not only to creating great agreements, but also to our general well-being. Finding a way out of this trap will save us time, energy and resources at work and in our relationships.

We will look at how to get out of this trap and develop greater self-awareness in a moment. First, let's explore why it is an inside-out job: how our own perception creates our reality, not the other way round.

You will see that this applies to any personal or professional activity where a final result is delivered at the end of a given period, such as the result of an election or a company's annual return. This example involves football. I was working with a Grade 9 class, helping to bring this 'inside-out' understanding of performance into the students' school lives. One of the students suddenly grasped the concept and explained it in relation to a recent, fiercely fought football game between two local teams. He explained how when his team won the North London Derby game by 3–1 the week before, the two opposing sets of fans had a completely different experience of the result, even though they were watching the same game. It wasn't the game or the football players who inspired these reactions in their fans, but rather the fans themselves who created an emotional response based on personal beliefs and their own experiences of the teams, this match and previous matches. While football is an obvious example of how some people can experience powerful emotions based on personal beliefs, when we look closely we see that this effect is visible in all aspects of our daily lives, from how we react to our partner leaving the milk out to how we feel about a negotiation partner's offer.

THINK ABOUT IT: UP IN THE AIR

If you have ever flown on an aeroplane you may have noticed a number of experiences of the same reality. For instance, despite flying regularly I still feel immense excitement every time I step on to a plane, and no number of reported accidents, lost planes or terrorist attacks seems to affect that experience. Yet many people feel quite differently.

One of my colleagues tells me that they are full of worrying thoughts before every flight. Their worries of what will happen during the flight build into a real anxiety as their flight approaches. The strange thing is that this person flies a lot and isn't afraid of flying itself, but of odour. They have close to a phobic response when they think they may be stuck next to someone who has poor hygiene or sweats a lot.

One of my teachers describes how she finds it impossible to enjoy a flight in the middle seat.

Clearly, these responses are the product of our own thoughts and emotions, rather than related to what's actually going on in the aeroplane cabin, but in the midst of experiencing these thoughts, they feel totally real.

Think for yourself. What experiences come to mind where you have had a very different reaction to someone else under the same circumstances? Can you see how your response was the product of your own interpretation of your thoughts and feelings?

Michael Neill, author of *Supercoach* and a personal coach to people in areas as wide as sport, entertainment, business and politics, talks movingly in his TED talk 'How To Be Awesomer' about the moment he realized that his thoughts, rather than his circumstances, were creating his reality. He credits this with creating a powerful shift in the way he was able to interact with and help others to collaborate. Neill calls this shift of understanding the 'Inside-Out Revolution' (which he explores in a book of the same name). What he demonstrates is that seeing that we are creating our reality from the inside-out is the best way to accelerate rapport, build genuine connection and accelerate collaboration. The more insight we have into this, the more connected we can be with what is really important for both us and the other party in a negotiation.

When we see that our opinions and perspectives have been created internally, it leaves us free to accept that others may see, or feel, differently. Having that awareness can be a very effective attribute to bring to our negotiations if we know how to use it. This is not to say we shouldn't listen to our thoughts and feelings at all, but rather when these are causing us distress or blocking progress, it's worth considering what is really driving the reaction. Might it be time for a new perspective? Wrapped up in our thoughts, we rarely solve problems creatively or develop the new ideas which are at the heart of brilliant agreements.

What I am suggesting is something that you will have seen before in your own life. When you stop concentrating on the first thought that comes to your mind, or your established position, you open up to fresh ideas and solutions. You may achieve this by consciously 'switching off' from thinking about something for a while, perhaps by engaging in a hobby or going for a walk, or by engaging with another person's perspective. You may achieve it when subconsciously switching off, relaxing or concentrating on another task. I've lost count of how many times I have had a brilliant idea as I was dropping off to sleep, or sitting in the bath drifting into a state of calm. Before the days of smartphones, I had a book by my bed to record my more practical ideas that came to me in these moments. Why is it that the best ideas come to us when we are not thinking?

For one thing, inspiration is more likely to come to you when you are not wrapped up in an existing thought pattern. Concentrating on one thought, such as the only way you can see a deal occurring, means you repeat that thought over and over again. Only once you take a break from it can you tap into your entire memory bank of experiences, your innate wisdom. Perhaps you'll make connections between previous negotiations' successes or failures and your current situation, or you'll remember something key about your partner's values. When we see that we don't need to take our own personal thinking so seriously, we are able to tap into more resourceful mindsets, where new ideas and solutions present themselves to us. If we are able to help our negotiation partner do the same, we are highly likely to come up with ideas together that will make a difference. If you can develop an understanding of how your mind really works, and how you create the experience that you see as your reality, you will give yourself a boost as a negotiator. And you will help the people you are negotiating with too, because by focusing on what really matters to you, not on your immediate reactions and thoughts, you will be able to point them towards a more grounded view of the situation.

try it now OBSERVING YOUR RESPONSES

Allow yourself to notice how your thoughts are the sole driver of your experience and understanding. Imagine you are watching a sports match on television. A goal is scored and the camera cuts to the crowd in the stadium.

What is actually happening as the ball goes in the net? What makes you interpret the crowd's response as tears of joy or sadness? How does your current mood, your knowledge of the season, and your thoughts about the sport and the teams involved affect your appreciation of the circumstances?

Conduct this experiment in different areas of your life and see if you can notice how in some situations your thinking will change quite quickly. Sometimes you may get new data that appear to impact your feelings, but notice how the thinking is always changing.

You may find that at different times it is easier to be aware and in control of your emotions and thought patterns, and at other times it seems inevitable that they will overwhelm you. Notice how your awareness of your thinking moves with your moods and makes your circumstances appear more or less 'real' accordingly.

As you begin to notice the role that your thinking – your perceptions, interpretations and feelings – is having on everyday situations you will start to appreciate the role it can play in your negotiations. The purpose is not to stop thinking or feeling – that's simply impossible – but when we notice the role it plays in the creation of our reality, we become free to accept new thoughts, new ideas and new ways of seeing things. This ability to have new thoughts, ideas and solutions seems directly proportionate to our ability to let go of old ones.

WHAT DOES THIS MEAN FOR OUR NEGOTIATIONS?

When you're in the middle of a negotiation, combining an awareness of your biases, beliefs and emotions with an effort to see things from the other party's perspective (Chapter 4) and factoring time-outs into the bargaining stage (Chapter 7) will help you to move past your gut reactions and initial offers.

One trap we can fall into when preparing or participating in a negotiation is to believe that the other party, their position or opinion is the source of our distress. As we've seen, even if it's our negotiation partner's intention to cause us distress (which hopefully isn't the case in most negotiations), our emotional response can only ever be created by us. We're responsible for feeling bad, or positive, about any situation. This may seem obvious and irrelevant to the act of negotiation, or you may wonder what you can do about your 'natural' response to the situation. Like in any other 'contact sport', understanding the role you play in creating your reality, awareness of your mood, and a desire to connect more deeply with your negotiation partner are important steps in your preparation and execution of deals. They allow you to use a hidden resource that is always in the background of every human interaction: creative energy.

The key to unlocking better deals may not be your technical preparation of the facts and figures, your actual care for your partner, or your ability to plan effectively. It may simply be your ability to respond intuitively and creatively in the moment you are crafting a deal, without getting caught up in thought – 'I must not give way on this variable', 'She is really intimidating', 'My boss will not be pleased if I don't get a deal done'. Of course I am not suggesting that all of your preparation is useless – otherwise the book would consist simply of this chapter – but you do need to allow that preparation to sit behind you as you engage with another person and talk to them about a deal. It's invaluable to feel prepared, but remember that the feeling of being prepared is self-generated, and what is critical is being present and able to craft agreement together with another person.

NEGOTIATING WITH PERSONAL AWARENESS

What may have become clear to you as you have been reading the chapter is that your ability to access your highest levels of creativity, your best ideas and your own wisdom are severely prejudiced by some of your rational thinking. While this may seem counterintuitive to many of us, the more I notice how my thinking actually works, the more I see how it drives all my feelings, and therefore all of my counterproductive behaviour as a negotiator. Whether you are a sports professional, an artist, or a banker, the greatest moments of 'flow', enhanced performance or connection, occur when you are truly present, without thoughts about the past or worries about the future to blur your headspace. The times when you are really available to connect properly with another human being are the times when the sense of 'I', fuelled by 'personal thinking', has been temporarily suspended, and your rational thinking has been replaced by something wider, more grounded and more present.

There is now a huge amount of research which suggests that certain meditative practices can promote this mindful state, but we all also have our own experiences of this state we can draw on. As a parent, I know that little comes from entering a discussion with my children or my spouse when I am upset, stressed or thinking in an agitated way. A busy mind creates routes for conflict and chaos, and rarely produces agreement, or even acceptance, in my household. By contrast, a settled mind often creates calm. Children are more likely to listen and to speak when they are calm, and to provide a space to be listened to. Resolution of issues soon follows when we listen and are really heard. Yet, the question I am always asked when this dawns on my clients is: 'Surely I can't just wait until I have a calmer mind to have conversations that matter, can I?' The question should really be: 'Can I afford to waste time having conversations that matter when my mind is full of unhelpful thinking?'

We do get to choose when we handle and discuss the most sensitive or challenging issues. Our feelings act as an inbuilt barometer that tells us whether our current thinking is likely to be a help or a hindrance to the discussion we are facing. When we understand this, we can schedule conversations appropriately or, during the course of a negotiation when it seems our negative emotions and unhelpful thinking are driving us too hard, we can call a time-out. Real collaboration with someone else is often accompanied by a warm, connected and grounded feeling; if this feeling isn't present we can ask ourselves whether we are really in the right state of mind to negotiate with another person.

However, as well as scheduling our discussions for a time when we're feeling calmer and calling time-outs when needed, we can also work on developing an awareness of our inside-out thinking, to help us see beyond our thoughts and feelings, and to help us be present in negotiations and connect with our negotiation partners. This means that we use that barometer of feelings, but we see that all it measures is our current mood, *not* what's actually happening. Once we appreciate that any negative, anxious or difficult feelings are only ever a result of our thinking, an internal reaction, we realize that an alternative is always there. So, stop taking your insecure thinking seriously, and allow yourself to get back to the clear thinking that is more likely to produce a positive outcome and a stronger connection. After all, to be a better negotiator, you simply need to be a better connector, and the main thing getting in the way of connecting with others is usually you.

This is important: there is no major change you need to make in order to reset your thinking. All you need to do is use your increased awareness to notice that it is your thinking which is causing the feelings, not the situation or elements from your external environment. Realizing this will help you to put aside unhelpful thoughts and moods, allowing for more creative, collaborative ideas to form the foundations of your agreements.

CHECKLIST FOR UNDERSTANDING THE OPERATING SYSTEM

1. Do you sometimes feel that the circumstances in your life are creating your feelings?

2. Can you see how sometimes your feelings vary when faced with the same circumstances at different times?

3. Do you ever notice how your best ideas come when you're not concentrating on finding a solution?

4. Have you noticed how you seem to connect instantly with some people, places and projects? What kind of thoughts and feelings were present, or absent, when you made those connections?

5. Are your thoughts and emotions getting in the way of your being present in the negotiations or agreements you are involved in?

6. How can you help yourself connect more to the person you are working with to reach agreement?

CHAPTER 10

Understanding Personality Traits for Better Negotiations

In order to connect and collaborate most effectively with another person, it is worth thinking about them as an individual, and exploring how their own unique personality may affect the way they are likely to collaborate with you. In this chapter, I will show you how understanding the specific aspects, or traits, of personality that you and your partner have will help you craft better agreements. We will see how great negotiators are able to adapt to and connect with others through a better understanding of their own and their partner's personalities. We will also look at how an understanding of the specifics of personality – the particular aspects of personality that you and your partner prefer – will enable you to flex your own style more effectively and adapt in order to connect with others of different personality types when you are negotiating.

Why is it useful to understand personality traits when negotiating? Sandra Proctor, negotiation trainer and an early mentor of mine, introduces the idea of Four Types of Negotiator. Her programme explores the role that your negotiation type – Expressive Negotiator, Driving Negotiator, Amiable Negotiator or Analytical Negotiator – plays in how you negotiate. Proctor demonstrates how understanding the Four Types of Negotiator enables you to see which styles you and your partner use most readily, and in developing this understanding, you can then focus on which aspects of your personality you need to tone down or tune up in order to connect most effectively with the other party.

At a basic level, a Driving Negotiator will be more outcome-focused, outgoing and concentrated in their approach. An Expressive Negotiator will be more sociable, idea-focused and flexible. An Amiable Negotiator will be more people-focused, adaptable and gentle, and an Analytical Negotiator will be more practical, detail-focused and reflective. These Negotiation Types each have their own ways of preparing, discussing, proposing, bargaining and agreeing. For example, Expressive Negotiators tend to like to jump in quickly and improvise. They enjoy the flexible approach and the interaction that comes with negotiating without too much preparation. Analytical Negotiators, on the other hand, prefer a more structured approach and value order and process. So a negotiation between people of these two Types is likely to create tension unless the parties work to complement and accommodate each other's preferred working styles.

I went on a negotiation skills course with Proctor in 1999, and I was soon able to see that I could adapt and connect with my negotiation partner more effectively by noticing how my style contrasted with or complemented theirs. I remember realizing quickly thereafter that one of my main contacts was much more Analytical than me, and so I toned down my more Expressive elements and included some more process-driven variables to move forward our deal. From having been a 'difficult' person to deal with, I was soon connecting well with this customer, and doing more business together as a result. So, understanding personality, and being able to measure personality in some way, is a useful tool to have under your belt as a negotiator.

FINDING YOUR SPARK: ARCHETYPES AND ASPECTS OF PERSONALITY

The roots of psychometrics – the measurement of aspects of a person's personality – stretch back more than 2,500 years, to when Hippocrates put forth the idea of the four humours: a system of four elements linked to human health, which divided people into phlegmatics, melancholics, sanguines and cholerics. While Hippocrates focused on health, his four humours map closely on to the modern theories of personality, from Carl Jung's eight personality types (developed in the early 20th century) to the

Myers-Briggs Type Indicator (MBTI) – which was widely used between the 1950s and 90s, and is still used by many businesses today – to Proctor's Four Types of Negotiator.

Traces of the humours can also be seen in the Four Personality Archetypes that underpin the model of personality classification we're looking at in this chapter. This model, called Lumina Spark, is a new approach to psychometrics devised by Stewart Desson, a business psychologist and consultant at the University of Westminster. It is grounded in the empirical evidence base of the 'Big Five' approach to measuring personality traits and has proven to be far more useful and effective than older methods when it comes to the application of psychometrics in the business world. I favour this approach because while it avoids the kind of pigeonholing that suggests you must be *either* an extrovert or an introvert (as often occurs in popular systems like MBTI), it does show how a combination of the aspects of your personality points you towards one of the Four Personality Archetypes.

The Four Archetypes match Proctor's Four Types of Negotiator, and provide an overarching framework for thinking about human personality, before adding depth with an additional Eight Aspects of Personality. The Four Archetypes are Commanding Red (like our Driving Negotiator), Inspiring Yellow (Expressive Negotiator), Empowering Green (Amiable Negotiator) and Conscientious Blue (Analytical Negotiator). These simple archetypes each involve a mixture of personality traits. The aim of this model is to give you a clear and simple concept that will help you to recognize your preferences, strengths and weaknesses – both in your broader personality and the personalities of the people around you at work and home, as well as in your and others' negotiation styles.

I have been using it for the past five years in my workshops and people find that having an understanding of both the specific aspect of personality that they and their partner use, and the overall Personality Archetypes that they tend towards, helps them to make a difference in their businesses and personal relationships. If you can get a grasp here of the Aspects of Personality you have a preference for, and therefore the Personality Archetypes you exhibit, you too will find that you can 'speed read' your negotiation partner more effectively, allowing you to adapt and connect with greater ease and better outcomes.

Let's look first at the Eight Aspects that make up your personality and will affect your preferred negotiation style.

THE EIGHT ASPECTS OF PERSONALITY

What appeals to me about the model that Stewart created with his team is that you can easily understand these eight aspects and therefore you will be able to recognize these aspects in yourselves and others.

It may be helpful to think about each of the following aspects as points on a wheel. Some traits will appear to have an opposite, such as Introversion and Extraversion, which face one another across the wheel. However, being on opposite sides does not make the traits mutually exclusive. Indeed, as the diagram on page 155 shows, we measure each aspect independently; so you might be high in the Introversion Aspect but also show some tendencies towards Extraversion. It's not a case of one or the other but rather a blend of tendencies and preferences. You may find, for instance, that you show preferences for very different aspects if you measure your whole personality, versus if you just focus on your home personality or work personality.

By understanding how you use these aspects, and which of these aspects your negotiation partners tend towards, you will be able to see how you can tone down certain aspects of your personality or tune up other aspects to lead to better working relationships.

BIG PICTURE THINKING

The Big Picture Thinking Aspect is about creativity. Looking at things in a unique way, people with a high Big Picture Thinking score are often visionaries. They look beyond the reality of 'what is' towards 'what could be'. They want to make improvements and shake up the status quo. These individuals will champion their ideas, even if it means introducing changes of dramatic proportions. In addition, they are not afraid to speak up even if others may consider their ideas strange.

DOWN-TO-EARTH

The Down-to-Earth Aspect is about knowing how to make projects manageable. People who are strong in this aspect dissect projects into smaller pieces and focus on the details. This attention to detail makes them very skilful at producing consistent and accurate work. They assess things in the light of their experience, preferring to utilize approaches that have worked for them in the past. They can be very even-minded and careful when accepting change initiatives and are likely to have a reputation for being more traditional in their methods.

EXTRAVERTED

The Extraverted Aspect is about enjoying working alongside other people. Individuals who are strong in this aspect have no trouble approaching new people and telling them about their thoughts and ideas. When they're thinking about something they like to voice their opinion and know that their voice is heard. People high in this aspect enjoy having new conversations just to see where they might lead. They can be sentimental and often display their feelings openly; when they're happy everyone will notice. They can be seen as the life of the party, exuding enthusiasm and always confident enough to speak up in a group.

INTROVERTED

Somebody high in Introversion is likely to be seen as private and level-headed, with a desire to keep their feelings under wraps. This can make them appear quiet and serious. They will think before they voice their opinions or act upon ideas, especially when they are in a group setting. They are measured and take a serious approach to work, controlling displays of excitement. They produce great results when they can work independently, as they often do not find the opportunity to speak up in a crowd. They are listeners who take into consideration other people's ideas and input before offering their own opinions.

PEOPLE-FOCUSED

The People-Focused Aspect is visible in someone who is willing to adapt their stance to accommodate others. They're not overly outspoken and avoid opportunities to express negative feedback. They are trustworthy and like to trust others. They seek harmony and approval from others, and may be known as peacemakers. They acknowledge others in a team, and appreciate their contributions.

They value other people's ideas but may be modest and uncomfortable with receiving praise themselves. They readily see the world from other people's perspectives, making them appear considerate and courteous.

OUTCOME-FOCUSED

The Outcome-Focused Aspect can apply to someone who is objective, rational, views themself as successful and enjoys competition. When faced with a challenge they take the logical route and a direct approach to communication, which is very 'to the point'. They are not afraid of conflict and can be tough negotiators because they prioritize the outcome over others' feelings. They are good at arguing their point in order to share their opinions. When others communicate with them, they will value their well-considered ideas. They dislike waffle.

DISCIPLINE-DRIVEN

The Discipline-Driven Aspect is evident in someone who utilizes self-discipline and demonstrates precision and punctuality. They tend to start work early and avoid last-minute deadlines. They take time management seriously – both their own and that of others. They think carefully before taking action and they take their commitments very seriously. They are very consistent in the application of their work ethic. They like to establish clear written objectives and work purposefully towards goals they have set. They are very organized and methodical, enjoying planning and scheduling what needs to be completed. They prefer to work in an ordered and structured environment.

INSPIRATION-DRIVEN

The Inspiration-Driven Aspect is present in someone who is flexible. They let the work pace develop naturally until a final objective becomes clear, and they like to let the direction emerge from an evolving situation. They are easy-going and are able to work loosely with processes. They use their gut instinct to make quick choices, using the pressure of approaching deadlines to push them into action. They take risks by bending rules and traditions, in order to achieve something that will be unique.

try it now YOUR EIGHT ASPECTS

Use the descriptions of the Eight Aspects to uncover which preferences you think you have. Give yourself a score of between 1 and 10 for each of the aspects, where 1 means you see very little of yourself in an aspect and 10 means you feel it describes you exactly. Feel free to choose aspects that are seemingly opposite. Many people are able to use opposite qualities in different aspects of their lives or at different times; why not you?

If, however, you are feeling that you have strengths in all areas, take a sense check. Are you really so well rounded? (If so, well done. There may be a role for you in the next X-Men movie!)

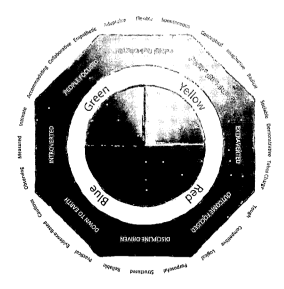

THE FOUR PERSONALITY ARCHETYPES – YOUR NEGOTIATION COLOUR STYLES

Now that we have a picture of our Eight Personality Aspects, we can narrow this down to Four Personality Archetypes, represented by the four colours, blue, green, yellow and red. Getting an idea of which archetype(s) best represent you will really help you to see how you approach negotiations and will thereby allow you both to play to your strengths and to work around your weaknesses. Recognizing the dominant archetype of your negotiation partner will give you great insight into how the negotiation is likely to unfold and how you can facilitate a productive negotiation by tuning up or toning down complementary or jarring aspects of your preferred style.

It's important to note that the model doesn't suggest that you will fall neatly into one colour type. Rather, most people will contain elements of all four colours to varying degrees. Recognizing this will help you to be more flexible in how you approach negotiations, playing up aspects of each colour as suits the individual you're negotiating with.

CONSCIENTIOUS BLUE – THE ANALYTICAL NEGOTIATOR

The blue archetype is defined by combining the aspects of Introversion, being Down-to-Earth and being Discipline-Driven. This often leads to a person with highly tuned organization skills, high reliability and attention to detail. Those who use a lot of this archetype are good listeners and observers, and tend to make objective decisions based on the evidence at hand.

The downside: this tendency towards empiricism can sometimes take the form of fussy, bureaucratic tendencies, and they can sometimes find themselves unable to make a decision due to 'information overload'.

Negotiating with a Conscientious Blue

The Analytical Negotiator is highly motivated by detail and factual elements of the deal. They reject personal approaches in the main and prefer to discuss tangible and practical details. They like to plan, so they are well-prepared negotiators, although their tendency to focus on detail and their reflective qualities mean that they may need time to consider proposals, and they may get bogged down by the detail, particularly if you don't give them enough time to analyse it properly.

DO

- Be well prepared and show it

- Be prepared to share details of your calculations where possible

- Stick to a process and communicate that you are doing so

- Establish clear timelines and be fastidious about sticking to them

- Provide practical data-driven examples of how the deal will work

- Listen carefully and allow plenty of time for reflection.

DON'T

- Try to wing it

- Be too 'Big Picture' in your approach; stick to the facts

- Change your plan too easily or get caught up with new ideas

- Try to introduce variables that are too creative, or unproven

- Speak too much or too quickly

- Try to make it too personal – keep your physical and emotional distance.

EMPOWERING GREEN – THE AMIABLE NEGOTIATOR

The green archetype is defined by empathy and people-skills. It contains a combination of Introversion, People Focus and being Inspiration-Driven. Amiable Negotiators work well with others and are able to appreciate multiple points of view. They are often perceived as a positive, calming influence within their organization.

The downside: this kind of sociability can make it difficult for them to function outside of a group dynamic, and they may find themselves taking on more work than they can manage due to being unable to say 'no' to anyone.

Negotiating with an Empowering Green

The Amiable Negotiator is motivated by people and cooperation, so will be interested in how the deal serves the people around them. They prefer to take a more cooperative approach, so will be more open and flexible in their approach. As they share the aspect of Introversion with the Analytical Negotiator, they will also need time to reflect, and won't like being pushed into making quick decisions, especially as they will want to consult with others first.

DO

- Focus on how the proposal will impact the people involved (whether that's within their or your organization, their clients or even their family members)

- Use real examples of the ways in which other people have benefited from your product or service

- Allow time for more reflective and personal conversations during the process

- Plan for an element of flexibility and welcome collaboration

- Listen and allow the person time to reflect

- Include creative variables, particularly ones that benefit other people.

DON'T

- Try to stick too rigidly to your plan

- Expect to move the process on too quickly

- Use too much detail or factual information to persuade

- Reveal too much of your competitive side (if you have one)

- Ignore the people in the process

- Be too direct or blunt.

INSPIRING YELLOW – THE EXPRESSIVE NEGOTIATOR

The yellow archetype is present in the 'fun' members of the office. It contains a combination of Extraversion, Big Picture Thinking and being Inspiration-Driven. They're spontaneous, imaginative and often the ones who offer solutions no-one else would have considered. They are socializers and adept at lightening the mood when necessary.

The downside: their fun-loving nature can work to their detriment, as they often show a tendency to be poorly organized and easily distracted.

Negotiating with an Inspiring Yellow

New ideas and creative thinking motivate the Expressive Negotiator. They enjoy engaging in the negotiation process when they are allowed to have input into making the deal different, and they enjoy brainstorming together to solve obstacles along the way. They are inspired by new ideas, and are prepared to throw caution to the wind to try out new ideas in the process.

DO

- Allow time for discussion face-to-face

- Be prepared to be flexible in your approach

- Listen to and encourage their creativity

- Prepare yourself, but don't expect them to

- Start with the big idea, and allow them to buy into this first

- Be descriptive and enthusiastic in your language and style.

DON'T

- Focus too much on facts or details

- Expect them to read everything you've sent them

- Try to stick too rigidly to a structure

- Ignore their ideas

- Present your idea as one that is already fixed

- Leave them with follow-up tasks that are not clearly defined.

COMMANDING RED – THE DRIVING NEGOTIATOR

The red archetype is all about action. It combines Extraversion with Outcome Focus and being

Discipline-Driven. They are decision-makers and go-getters, usually the first to take charge in a group. They are highly competitive and motivated and will tend to go far in their chosen careers as a result.

The downside: this directness can come at the expense of social skills and they may be perceived by others as overly aggressive and insensitive.

Negotiating with a Commanding Red

The Driving Negotiator likes to win in their negotiations and is more comfortable with conflict than many of the other archetypes. They like to get on with things at a fast pace and enjoy making quick decisions in order to achieve their desired outcomes. While they are not naturally the most flexible or collaborative people, if you can show them the value of cooperation to them or their business, they will quickly get on board with a collaborative approach.

DO

- Stick to the facts

- Focus on outcomes

- Allow them to be in control of the pace of the negotiation, and be prepared to move at a fast pace

- Expect them to make quick decisions

- Show them the next steps and how to take them.

DON'T

- Get competitive or try to win an argument
- Get annoyed if they keep you waiting or try to dominate you
- Get into too much detail
- Focus on feelings
- Be too conceptual, or focused on ideas
- Expect them to involve too many others in the process of agreeing the deal.

All four archetypes have their upsides and downsides, but no-one is necessarily better than the others, nor correlates with being more effective or collaborative as a negotiator. It's only when a person overextends their strengths in one particular colour that it starts to become a weakness. By appreciating the differences between people and learning to read others, it's possible to adapt your negotiation style to best suit the kind of person you are collaborating with.

try it now FINDING YOUR COLOURS

Using your scores for each of the Eight Aspects from the exercise on page 154, combine them to see how much you regularly use each of the Four Personality Archetypes. In completing both this and the previous exercise, you may even want to focus on how you use these personalities when you are negotiating specifically. If you've done the exercise in relation to your broader life, how do your general and negotiating personalities differ?

Conscientious Blue Archetype – Analytical Negotiator

Discipline Drive   _____

Down-to-Earth   _____

Introversion   _____

TOTAL   _____

Empowering Green Archetype – Amiable Negotiator

Introversion   _____

People Focus   _____

Inspiration Drive   _____

TOTAL   _____

Inspiring Yellow Archetype – Expressive Negotiator

Inspiration Drive   _____

Big Picture Thinking   _____

Extraversion   _____

TOTAL   _____

Commanding Red Archetype – Driving Negotiator

Extraversion   _____

Outcome Focus   _____

Discipline Drive   _____

TOTAL   _____

try it now

Think of a person you are negotiating with and go through each of the Eight Aspects of their personality. Mark them between 1 and 10 on how you think they use each aspect. Using this information, list which two of the Four Personality Archetypes are strongest in them.

How does your use of the Colour Archetypes compare to your negotiation partner's? How may that cause tension when you are negotiating? What can you do to tune up or tone down aspects of your personality to adapt more effectively with this partner?

The more you think of how you can adapt and connect with others by looking at how you are different, the easier you will find to get on with people in many walks of life. Ultimately I have found that there are very few 'difficult' people, just 'different' people. Understanding these differences has helped me craft many relationships and agreements that go beyond what I may have imagined. I trust this kind of reflection and adaptive action will do the same for you.

THE VALUE OF FLEXIBILITY

The idea of a fixed personality that is established during your childhood, stays with you forever and cannot be adjusted is not one that Desson's team has a lot of truck with. As part of a growing group of psychologists who take a 'humanistic' approach to psychology, they have produced evidence which suggests that people are able to adapt aspects of their personalities over the course of their lifetime and in response to their experiences. My experience as a trainer supports the view that every individual does have the ability to adjust aspects of their *behaviour*, regardless of the personality preferences they most commonly use. The flexible view of personality is also supported by a recent study by Nathan Hudson and R. Chris Fraley at the University of Illinois at Urbana-Champaign, which produced evidence that, when motivated to do so, individuals could change specific aspects of their personality and boost their usage of a particular personality trait.

The importance of these findings is that with a strong understanding of basic personality traits, you can tune up or tone down any aspect with a bit of effort. Even if your personality preference is largely fixed (i.e. you find it easiest and prefer to be an Empowering Green), behaviour is something we can choose from moment to moment (i.e. you can work to exhibit Commanding Red behaviours when needed). Understanding the behaviour that goes with a particular personality trait will enable you to make the right adjustments to your behaviour in order to connect with the person you are negotiating with more effectively.

CHECKLIST FOR UNDERSTANDING AND USING PERSONALITY TRAITS IN NEGOTIATION

1. Are you clear about how you use the Eight Aspects of your personality?

2. Can you see which aspects of your personality you may overuse in negotiation situations and therefore need to tone down?

3. Can you see which of the Four Personality Archetypes you use most in negotiations? Does your dominant colour vary in different negotiations?

4. Have you noticed how your negotiation partner is using the Eight Aspects of their personality? Are they dominant in a particular Colour Archetype?

5. How may you tone down certain aspects of your personality to connect more effectively with specific parties?

6. How may you change the way you prepare and propose agreements to adapt your style to specific partners you have identified as different to you?

CHAPTER 11

Using the Seven Steps at Home

In this chapter, we will explore how you can apply the Seven Steps of Negotiation to conflicts in your home life; how you can see past your own point of view, feelings and beliefs; and how you can bring your understanding of your own and others' personalities into creating greater harmony with your family and friends. One of the reasons that I wrote this book was because of the strength of feedback I receive about how using the tools and techniques from my professional negotiation course has created impact at home and transformed personal relationships.

I need to start with a reminder of something that can often get buried under the everyday routine or forgotten in the rush of emotions that can accompany family disputes: whatever tools you use, and whatever techniques you employ, your family are human. Just like you, they will vary greatly in their levels of awareness, and day-to-day their moods will affect their ability to see how their thinking is really impacting their feelings. So, just like you there will be times that, despite the agreements you have in place, they will act up and break promises. And, without making any excuses for your behaviour, despite your great intentions, you may also do the same. The purpose of this chapter is not to eliminate negative feelings, thoughts or practices, but to minimize the impact they have on your behaviour. Whether you're having communication issues with your partner, working on improving your kids' behaviour, managing care for your elderly parents, or planning a holiday with friends, negotiation skills can help you to minimize negative thoughts and practices and to create greater harmony, trust and understanding.

The idea of applying a formal framework to settling conflicts at home may strike you as odd, but bear with it. You may be surprised by how much you can improve your relationships and home life by giving yourself the time to try it out.

STEPS ONE TO THREE: PREPARING TO NEGOTIATE AT HOME

If we recall the seven steps to successful agreements we remember that the first three steps fall into preparation.

1. Prepare yourself.
2. Prepare your plan.
3. Understand your partner's point of view.

What often trips us up at home is that we get little time to really prepare. We jump into, or are sometimes thrown into, discussions about plans, the weekend, chores or homework without a moment to think. I am often corralled into giving opinions, ideas and solutions in the hallway, over soup or over the phone. My children are able to use a simple strategy espoused by the author and military strategist Niccolò Machiavelli in 1520 in *The Art of War*: 'Divide and Rule'. They ask me whether they can have a snack or an ice cream, often having already asked their mum. They may even imply that their mum has said it would be okay. Or they ask me about plans for the weekend at a time that they know I can't check in with their mum.

So, the first step is a simple one that we all ignore at our peril: in any negotiation, *prepare first*. Prepare in your team – whether that's your partner/spouse, your siblings or housemates. Make sure you and your partners are aligned before you talk to the other party – even, and perhaps especially, if the 'other party' are children. (Let's not forget Millie's negotiating power.) If we are comfortable giving ourselves time to prepare for complex negotiations at work, we should also give ourselves time at home, and we should be prepared to tell our children, partners or parents that we need time to reflect before we will discuss the issue with them.

KNOWING WHEN TO NEGOTIATE WITH OTHERS

One of the things that you will need to agree before you
seek to craft agreements with your family or friends is
the areas in which you are prepared to negotiate. Some
parents tell me clearly that they will never negotiate with
their children because they believe that it's their house,
their rules. If that is the case in your house, and your
children stick to your rules, then this isn't relevant to you.
In our home we are attempting to teach our children how
to feel empowered, and so we are open to negotiation
in a fair number of areas, and we want them to play an
active part in making the rules and crafting the agreements. The truth is, with some pretty headstrong kids,
and having realized early on that I can't *force* my kids
to do anything, I've realized that I have to negotiate if I
want them to do stuff when I am not there, and do stuff
they don't want to do.

That said, in all areas of work, life and love there need to be Red Lines, constants and non-negotiables. You need to be clear with everyone around you as to what those non-negotiables are. Child psychologists tell us that children particularly value clear boundaries and feel more secure when they know what is clearly beyond negotiation and what isn't. In our house there are some things that are clearly non-negotiable. Devices at the table. Weekday bedtimes. Turning over the TV when Spurs are playing. You may choose to have more non-negotiables, and like us you may even choose to open up some of your non-negotiables to negotiation once a year.

For example, we held a discussion about bedtimes this summer when our youngest asked for it because she felt the current structure was unfair. Saffi felt her bedtime was earlier than most children's at school, and she felt that the current differentiation between her bedtime and her older siblings, Ziggy and Yasmin, was too great (30 minutes). She also felt that the restrictions on screen time were being unfairly applied because Ziggy was being allowed to watch football in the evenings with me, and Yasmin was using her computer for her homework. It was a great discussion, and we were all well prepared for it. It was very cute; the kids had even prepared a whole list of resources we could use, including websites, video clips and a summary of their research conducted with their friends. My wife, Jools, and I had also managed to in your thinking, the more likely it is that you will create an agreement which benefits all.

AGREEING A TIME TO NEGOTIATE/DISCUSS

Once you have seen that there is an area that you need to discuss, it is important to find enough time to prepare. In truth, at home we don't call this process 'negotiation' – I suspect my kids don't even know what the word means. But they know that if they have a substantial issue that they want to discuss, neither Mum nor Dad will discuss it with them until they have discussed it together first. And because I realize that I often need time to let ideas come to me without forcing them, we all know that we need to plan our discussions in advance. The process of setting a time to discuss an issue and the act of preparing to make an agreement will make a difference to the way the issue is resolved. Why is this?

People have often said to me that it seems crazy to plan a time to have an argument. They say that when they are angry or upset with their children or partner, they don't want to wait, and they can't see that it's practical to arrange a time to hammer the issue out. It seems ridiculous to them to plan a time to disagree. Well, it is! If you are seeking disagreement, then do it when you are gripped by annoyance, irritation or anger. Discuss it when your head is full of what's wrong, and you haven't yet seen what can be right. Talk when you are still gripped by your insecurity, rather than wrapped up in love. But don't expect it to go well. Don't expect your partner to see your point of view, and don't expect your kids to feel loved or valued. If you have been brought up with a model of parenting that involved anger and coercion, then feel free to repeat that pattern, and bully or psychologically coerce your children and lovers, to see your point of view, but don't expect to have extraordinary relationships, and don't anticipate that your family will thank you for it.

When you are gripped by your own frame of mind, and believe that something or someone else is wrong, and that you are right, it's not the time to craft collaborative agreements. Give yourself time to see what is really going on. Give yourself time to think of variables that can add value to both sides, and to come at the issue from the other person's point of view. Once you see the issue with new perspective, it's often so easy to get agreement it can be hard to understand why you disagreed in the first place. If you make it clear in the planning stage that this is what you are doing, it will have even better results.

Tell whoever you're negotiating with – let's say your children – that you are going to discuss all the options with your partner first, and will do your best to see it from their point of view. Explain to them that you will first prepare, and expect them to do so as well, and then you will discuss all the issues together. Make it clear that you may not get agreement in the first discussion, and that you and your partner may need to go away to discuss and come up with a proposal after this initial discussion. While this may not always be necessary, it is good practice to let the other party know the process you are working with. By stating this clearly in advance, you signal that you are prepared to collaborate, and that you will need to discuss with your partner during the process. This is no different than flagging in a professional negotiation that you may need to seek agreement from a 'higher authority' or seek a time-out to get clarification of an issue.

EQUALITY IN PARENT-CHILD RELATIONSHIPS

A word on equality. Some people tell me that they don't want their children to feel they are equal in their home and that they feel they as parents should 'rule the roost'. I can understand what they mean. They tell me that children's pre-frontal lobes are not developed enough to be able to make decisions. If this is true for you or your children, then don't negotiate with them. The same goes in your other relationships. If you don't want to be equal, don't negotiate collaboratively. But again, don't expect to experience the benefits of being in a collaborative relationship. I am not saying that you should let your children negotiate in every areas of their life, but I am saying here that home is a great place to teach the principles of collaboration.

STEP FOUR: DISCUSSION – LISTENING AND BEING LISTENED TO

As you may remember, the stage after preparation is discussion: discussing the options openly with the other party and finding out which possibilities are on or off the table for agreement. In business we often start this phase by reconfirming our willingness and intention to make an agreement; in relationships we should do the same, but the result may be a little more personal. If you are discussing something challenging with your children, partner or other loved one, remember that this is not a business deal. It is personal.

So, be personal. Share your feelings, reiterate your love, and express how important it is that you find a way together to live happily and harmoniously, or to get through a serious disagreement. Give time for everyone to speak, and to be heard. Think about either formally or informally applying the Co-Active Listening model (page 76). That is, let people speak, and give them time to really express themselves. Then let them know you've understood by repeating it back to them and asking: 'Did I get that right? Is there anything I missed?'

Until you have all had a chance to listen and be listened to, it will be hard to get an agreement that works for all. Bear in mind that this can take time with families. Allowing your family members time to prepare, and ensuring that they have space to do this, will often produce a breakthrough on its own. You may find that once you have all spoken and been listened to, the solutions become obvious to you as a team. In my family, when we sit together and speak like this we use a symbolic object (we call it 'the talking stone'), to pass around. When a family member has the stone, they're the centre of our attention, and until they put it down, they can't be disturbed. Whether you use a talking stone or not, ensuring that everyone is heard will be the cornerstone of making agreements that work in your home. If you're the one driving the negotiation, you may find that this role comes to you – stepping in to ensure that everyone has their turn and isn't interrupted.

STEP FIVE: PROPOSING THE SOLUTION

In business it's often a good idea to be the one to make the first move, and state your proposal first. However, when negotiating in families, allowing others the opportunity post-discussion to try to craft the final agreement is often a great idea. Sometimes you will realize that it is definitely your job; for instance, you may want to discuss it with your partner before you present the family with your final solution. In other cases, allowing the other person the chance to prepare the final agreement will make sure they are fully engaged and have a better understanding of what is needed from them, and everyone else. This can work particularly well with children. Often the solution will come to you collaboratively as you hear everyone's point of view and you realize what is possible.

STEP SIX: BARGAINING

In family situations if you have truly heard each other, you may largely propose agreements that work for all without needing to go back and forth through a process of bargaining. You may, however, have concessions you are prepared to make on certain conditions; so it's important to remember the value of *if* at this stage. Sometimes you will have to create additional terms in your agreements that are conditional on certain circumstances. For example, just a few days after agreeing our bedtimes, we found a reason to allow the children to stay up an extra 30 minutes later (Spurs playing a critical game). Fortunately, we had already agreed that in special circumstances *if* the children do their reading and bedtime preparations before their official bedtime, *then* they can extend their time out of bed.

At home, just like in business, remember that everything can be negotiable if you are prepared to look for variables to exchange that make it work for both parties. This attitude is key to meeting everyone's needs, and if you do this explicitly at home, you create an environment where children and adults can express their needs and expect to collaborate naturally. Using the phrase 'If you ..., then I ...' will help make this bargaining conditional, and will demonstrate the mutually beneficial element of the arrangement.

'If you help me load the dishwasher, then I will complete your homework diary.'

'If you clean the car, then I will take you and your friends to the trampoline centre tomorrow.'

STEP SEVEN: AGREEMENT

There are some agreements with your partner that will be contractually binding, like a pre-nuptial agreement or matters of property, and many require a witness and lawyers, but they are few and far between. Earlier I mentioned that my wife and I have our wedding certificate displayed on the wall; in some homes you see public declarations of other commitments, such as agreements around how the children will behave. Some popular child psychologists and the TV 'expert' Supernanny suggest these are good ways to remind children of their commitments and ensure promises are kept. Certainly, getting one of the parties to write out the agreement and getting the other to agree it, either verbally or by means of a signature, is a good way to ensure that there is no ambiguity in what the agreement means. In my children's school the teachers do an exercise with the children to create agreements around behaviour at the beginning of the year, and it seems that how they are displayed plays a part in ensuring they are part of the culture in the classroom.

You may choose to mark your agreement verbally, to write it down and display it. Or you may choose to use a symbolic object to demonstrate both parties' commitment to the agreement, much like the tradition, which many cultures share, of wearing a wedding ring to signify commitment to a marriage.

THINK ABOUT IT: AGREEMENTS AT HOME

Are there any agreements in your personal life that would benefit from being more explicit in the way they are articulated? Perhaps you feel you're taking on too much of the household chores, relative to your partner or housemates, but you've never clearly discussed sharing these responsibilities. Or maybe you'd like to clarify to your child that they can only get access to certain hobbies or treats if they spend a set amount of time on their homework? Would you like more explicit agreements around how you spend the time you have together as a family? Do you want to start the process of negotiating these agreements so they can be written in a way that is clear? Is there a way of displaying the agreements you have that may act as an inspiration for the behaviour you want to encourage?

CHECKLIST FOR NEGOTIATING AT HOME

1. Do you see yourself as an equal in the relationship, and if not what can you do to make yourself feel more equal?

2. Are there really issues here that are negotiable, or are we talking about non-negotiables?

3. Have you decided on your Red Lines and what you want, intend to get and need (your WIN outcomes)?

4. Are you ready to collaborate to reach an agreement?

5. What variables have you considered that could be used to make the situation more attractive for either party?

6. Have you considered the situation from the other person's point of view? Have you understood what their wants, expectations and needs may be, and do you have a fertile Green Zone of Agreement?

7. Have you planned a set time in which to discuss the issue? And have you both had a chance to prepare?

8. Do you have enough variables to make sure the final agreement works for all?

9. How will you seal the agreement in a way that ensures you both know what you have agreed and are reminded of it?

CHAPTER 12

Avoiding Common Gambits Some Negotiators Use

One of the biggest challenges you will face as a negotiator are people who see it as their role to play games with you rather than collaborate. This may be something that stems from a company culture, or could be rooted in a personal belief system that you can't get through. If someone has been working towards win–lose as a negotiation strategy for many years, then your collaborative approach may appeal to some, but to others it may just look like a lamb is being led to the slaughter. When you are faced with this type of competitive negotiator it will help you to understand that they are neither trusting, nor trustworthy. While it's best to avoid people like this like the plague, if you need to negotiate with them it's good to know the tricks they may be using to create an advantage over you in their negotiations.

A gambit is a move designed to bring a later advantage to a competitor in a game of strategy, where the objective is win–lose. These strategies are often successful in the short term, so while they are of no use to us who seek real partnerships, they do create results for those who don't care for collaboration or long-term partnership. Some of these gambits are pre-planned and sometimes they appear almost randomly as a competitive negotiation partner pulls any trick out of their bag to get a win. Sometimes they don't even know they are doing it, it's become so inbuilt in people's behaviour. The challenge is that sometimes it's hard to tell between a gambit, and a genuine issue, so it's important to be able to spot them and do your best to breeze through the imbalances they seek to create.

You should know that all of the tactics covered below have at some time been taught to negotiators as strategies for success. Sometimes they're taught in training programmes, and sometimes they're passed along more subtly through watching others. The purpose of this section for you is to help you spot some of the most common gambits, so they don't put you off, or catch you off guard. I won't offer you any smart counters to these moves, for to do so would be to fall into the competitive trap. My advice is to ignore them and return to trying to find a solution that works best for both of you. If that's not possible above your Red Line, then walk away with dignity and pride and find someone else to do the deal with. Countering these kind of silly tricks will do no more than waste your time.

NIBBLING - 'THE COLUMBO'

This is a trick that works so often that it's a surprise you don't hear it more often. At the point of being close to agreement, one negotiator mutters the catchphrase of the 70s TV cop Columbo: 'Just one more thing ...' Just like Columbo, the aim here is to catch the other party off guard. The words may not be 'just one more thing', they may ask for another concession, free delivery, an extra day, another item. The point is that it is a carefully considered move. Most people who have worked carefully through a long negotiation won't want to start again, or risk failure, so they concede to the extra demand, feeling relieved it's the last step to the deal being closed. The challenge is that if you feel taken by it, you lose trust, respect and long-term collaboration is out the window.

I have fallen for this trick enough times: the car dealer who added a £250 delivery fee at the last minute, the bike hire company that added a charge for hiring a helmet only after I had signed the hire form, and the lawyer I mentioned earlier who insisted on having the photocopier with a stapling function as I was leaving (see page 112).

When you know you are being played, you get a choice. Accept, or say no, it all depends on what your Red Lines really are. When I said no to the car dealer, he called back within ten minutes to withdraw the request.

THE FLINCH

The sharp intake of breath, 'ouch' or shock gesture is a tactic that is designed to put you off guard and get you to reduce your request or make a concession. It's a simple power play, but my personal experience is that it is remarkably effective at achieving concession in a majority of cases. It has many guises, 'I just fell off my chair', 'I'm in shock', etc., but the gist is the same, a shift to the balance of power caused by the expression of surprise at the offer or request you have made.

Ignore it, or laugh it off. I recently sent a set of rubber floor mats to a contact who had repeated the 'I just fell off my chair' line to me for the second time in as many years. We laughed about it, and we moved on. When it's not possible to laugh off this kind of reaction, you just need to stay firm, repeat your reasonable offer and engage in a dialogue that gets back to finding out how you can find variables to make the agreement work for both of you.

THE RED HERRING

A red herring is an expression derived from a nasty tactic apparently used in fox hunting competitions, where one team drags a dead fish across the fox's path to distract the other team's dogs and put them on to a false trail. At the bargaining table it can be where one side brings up a minor point to distract the other side from the main issue. Sometimes this happens where a party insists on something that they don't really want, just so that when they concede, they will be able to get something in return.

For example, a customer asks for an early delivery or a specific time slot, even though it is not necessary for them, and then – when the company can't meet their delivery needs – asks for a discount on the delivery. Or it could be a buyer who asks for a specific colour of item that is not available and then asks for a price reduction when they don't get the colour they 'wanted'. When you suspect someone is playing an issue like this you have two choices. You can call them out on it and see if the issue is really that important, or you can try to set it aside and get back to the issues that are really important. As soon as you realize it could be a red herring, you are likely to pay it less attention and start to focus on what really matters to you both.

HIGHER AUTHORITY

When someone wants to stall a decision, or avoid a reasonable request, they may use the excuse that there is a higher authority they need to discuss the issue with. This may be to buy time, to extract a concession, or to put you off guard. It may, of course, not be a gambit but a genuine need either to consult someone else, or just to have time to reflect on the offer, like when I tell people I need to discuss an arrangement with my wife, when she might be fine for me to make the decision alone but I just want time to think. (Remember the importance of time-outs during the bargaining phase, as we discussed in Chapter 7?) You don't need to overanalyse this one, but offering to talk to the higher authority yourself – 'Do you want me to speak about it to your boss?' – often dissolves the issue straightaway if it's just a gambit.

THE RELUCTANT BUYER/SELLER

This gambit hopes to shift the balance of power by changing the person's belief in whether the buyer/seller wants to buy or sell. In this gambit the buyer pretends that they do not want the product or service, or don't value the variables being offered, in order to impact the confidence of the seller, and affect the way they set their price or respond to the offer. Or, the seller pretends that they do not really want to sell the product, or don't value the offer being made, in order to impact the confidence of the buyer, and affect the way they frame their offer. It fits into the mindset of my Booba, whom I mentioned earlier, who believed that 'enthusiasm is expensive'. My estate agent also believed we should have employed this gambit before putting in an offer for our house and was therefore annoyed when, on the first viewing, I told the owner that we loved it.

If you have a party in a negotiation who is saying

they are not keen on the deal in the first place, you fall victim to this tactic. You may then change your expectations to try to meet the other party's needs when they were in fact feigning disinterest.

I recently saw this tactic backfire when on holiday. A tourist enquired about a bungalow in the resort we were staying in, but in trying to lower the price he stated that he ideally wanted something altogether different. He seemed pleased with himself as he discussed with his partner how he had feigned that the room was a little basic, when actually it was perfect for them. However, when they turned up later with their bags and the bungalow had been let to someone else, I guess they realized that using the tactic, especially in peak season, had been a little short-sighted.

The point is that any of these tactics may seem appropriate in situations when you are trying to achieve a win–lose outcome. So, if you see them being employed in your own negotiations, you'll know that you haven't managed to create a collaborative approach to the negotiation.

My only advice if you think someone is playing the 'reluctant buyer' or the 'reluctant seller' is to call it out. Ask them whether they really want to do a deal (remember your agreement question – see pages 109–10). Don't enter into a negotiation unless you have a party who wants a deal; otherwise you may be working towards a deal that won't work for all of the parties.

THE BEST OF A BAD CHOICE

Be particularly wary of someone who is offering you two choices, both of which are disadvantageous to you, only one less so. It's a classic trick that is designed to lull you into taking the better of two bad choices.

> 'I can either deliver this in two weeks, or I will have to deliver after 10 o'clock at night.'

> 'You can take the one with the damaged box, or wait two weeks for a new delivery.'

> 'You can accept this low price for ten units, or I will only be able to buy one unit at a time.'

> 'Your place, or mine?'

As our minds like to choose what's best, we are moved towards avoiding the calamity of the worse option. Offer and ask for more options. Always.

GOOD COP/BAD COP

We know this gambit from the movies, and job interviews, but it's a really effective tactic if you want to put someone off guard, and persuade them to deal with the Good Cop over the Bad Cop. One person in the organization acts like a friend, and the other as a foe. Sometimes the nasty Bad Cop doesn't even appear in the room, but is present as a threat, mentioned in order to scare you into doing a deal with the 'nicer' Good Cop.

If you don't know it's coming it can be scary, like when I started a presentation to a large law firm following a clear brief. The Bad Cop started their act pretty quickly, and I was starting to lose confidence and energy. It seemed the brief was wrong and maybe they didn't need the kind of specifications we were proposing. But my boss was a seasoned pro and knew what was going on. He stood up and suggested we leave. He asked the Good Cop to settle their issues internally and then invite us back once the specification was clear. The tables turned very quickly with the Bad Cop shrinking into a shell and letting us continue with the presentation unabated.

try it now COUNTERING GAMBITS

This exercise is optional (as if the others weren't!) because it will only be helpful if you are often negotiating with people who you feel are using gambits to challenge your position.

Go through each of the gambits and note which ones you think you have encountered. List those you feel you are likely to encounter again and think about how you would respond to them in a way that promotes cooperation and redresses a balance of power. Your best response will often be a question rather than a statement, clarifying their intentions, calling out the trick, or putting the onus back on them to come up with a collaborative response.

There are many more gambits listed in other books on negotiation. By listing some of the most common ones in this chapter, I hope you will be able to notice when they are being used against you. The challenge with them all is to keep working towards collaboration. If you suspect you are being played, then it's probably best you walk away and find an honest party to deal with. Remember that *gambits are a signal, not a solution*.

CHECKLIST FOR AVOIDING GAMBITS

1. Do you trust the person you are negotiating with?

2. What could you do outside of the negotiation to increase the level of trust you have for the person you are negotiating with?

3. What can you do to increase the amount of trust they have in you?

This checklist is short because trust is all that matters in negotiations; working to build a foundation of trust will result in negotiations with less conflict and competition, and instead more cooperation and collaboration.

Can You Really Get More by Giving More?

Thank you for getting this far. Either you are a person who never gives up, you are still looking for a last gem of wisdom, or you've already seen some value in the simple ideas I have been sharing throughout this book. Maybe all three. I thank you because I know that by applying some of this timeless advice about cooperation, you have the opportunity to create ripples of positive action that can reach out far beyond one negotiation or one relationship, and far beyond what you're able to see. Every action produces a reaction; in our personal and professional lives we are constantly faced with choices about what kind of actions we will take, and what kind of reactions we will try to inspire. I am grateful that you see some possibility in the idea of collaborative negotiation because I have seen so many better relationships, better deals and better businesses because of people adopting an attitude of trying to make agreements that work for all. This chapter is intended to provide a short summary of what we have covered, and to remind you of how you can apply these principles in varied places to create a positive impact.

The fundamental premise of this book has been that

human beings, as social animals with varied skills and resources at hand, work better together, and that by harnessing our resources, we have the possibility to create a greater net output than if we use our resources solely to achieve our own aims. If we can craft collaborative agreements, we can provide results for the people around us that they couldn't have achieved without us, and we likewise achieve with their support outcomes we wouldn't have reached alone. Using this understanding, we are able to proactively work with others to generate ideas and agreements that use each other's strengths, resources and networks to the best ability.

We have to be proactive and rigorous in our approach and to apply a clear structure to both our preparation and our execution in order to succeed in our goals. The seven-step structure is, however, nothing without an attitude of collaboration at each step and the belief that by combining resources with your negotiation partner you can achieve more together than you would apart.

This is why the preparation stage is split into three distinct parts because attitude must come first. It's crucial to recognize our own perspective and ready ourselves mentally before doing the same for our partner. Preparing separately from both perspectives is much more likely to give you a view of the issues that will generate collaborative excellence.

People need to be heard in order to explore

possibilities, and so we saw that a critical stage in negotiations is questioning, listening and searching for creative variables that add extraordinary value to the deal. While these ideas may come in your preparation (steps one to three), they are more likely to come from open and effective dialogue (steps four to six). No holds-barred communication allows you to determine what the real issues are, and to work together to find variables that can be exchanged for mutual gain.

Exchange is ultimately the means by which negotiations yield value for all parties. Through the preparation, discussion and proposal stages we set up a Green Zone of Agreement that enables us to bargain effectively and exchange things of real value to each other. And because we are focused on making agreements that are clear and easy to execute, we saw that, in many cases, committing to these agreements on paper or in public is a useful way of finalizing what we want in a concrete way and of holding us to our promises.

REMEMBER THIS

Remember that value creation is the purpose of negotiation, as Stanford Professor Margaret Neale explains:

> Negotiation is about finding a solution to your counterpart's problem that makes you better off than you would have been had you not negotiated.

Beyond the formal, seven-step structure of negotiation, you now know that negotiation happens between humans, and so an understanding of the human experience is key to facilitating your agreements with others. You are likely to find that understanding more about the personality of the person you are negotiating with produces almost instant results.

Yet the biggest barrier to communication is never wholly outside us, caused by others' personalities or even circumstances. Instead, the biggest barrier is within us: caused by our perceptions, reactions and rationalizations. Awareness of how our own 'operating system' works, and the mechanics of our changeable reactions, enables us to take our own emotions and point of view less seriously and to see beyond them in the critical times when we need to connect with others. As we increase this awareness, we get to access our innate creativity, and discover solutions and ideas that come from beyond the narrowness of our own personal perspective. Understanding this fundamental link between our thinking, our moods and our ability to access our most productive peak states is a useful tool. For if we are gripped by insecure thinking or unproductive moods, we are unlikely to be able to collaborate effectively. You will see in the appendix some further reading to help you develop a deeper understanding of how this breakthrough in mindful thinking can make a difference to your experience of life and to your relationships.

I trust that you appreciate that you will never become a better negotiator, nor craft more collaborative agreements, simply by reading this book. It is only by applying some of the ideas that have inspired you into your day-to-day interactions that this effort can make a difference in your life. And so I look forward to hearing how you have applied what you have learned through reading this work.

Best of luck. The best is yet to come.

Recommended Reading

There are hundreds of other books on the shelves about negotiation, but we published this one to give a new view. A more collaborative view, and a more practical view. Here are more resources to help take your understanding further on the topics we covered in the book. This also includes further details of authors and books mentioned throughout.

Two books which have really helped me along my own way are *The Missing Link* and *The Enlightened Gardener* by Sydney Banks. Both are difficult to source, although they are available at sydneybanksproducts.com. Here are some other books that you should be able to find more easily and are well worth a read.

Burns, Chantal. *Instant Motivation: The Surprising Truth behind What Really Drives Top Performance* (FT Press, 2014).

Carlson, Richard. *Don't Sweat the Small Stuff: Simple Ways to Keep the Little Things from Taking over Your Life* (Hodder, 1998).

Cialdini, Robert. *Influence: The Psychology of Persuasion* (HarperBusiness, 2007, first published 1984).

Cramer, Garret. *Stillpower: Excellence with Ease in Sports and Life* (Beyond Words Publishing, 2012).

Fisher, Roger, William Ury & Bruce Patton. *Getting to Yes: Negotiating an agreement without giving in* (Random House Business, 2012, first published 1981).

Fromm, Erich. *The Art of Listening* (Constable, 1994).

Grant, Adam. *Give and Take: Why Helping Others Drives Our Success* (W&N, 2014).

Kennedy, Gavin. *Kennedy on Negotiation* (Routledge, 1997).

Manning, Ken, Robin Charbit & Sandra Krot. *Invisible Power: Insight Principles at Work* (Insight Principles, 2015).

Marcum, David, & Steven Smith. *Egonomics: What Makes Ego Our Greatest Asset (or Most Expensive Liability)* (Simon & Schuster, 2007).

Neill, Michael. *Supercoach: 10 Secrets to Transform Anyone's Life* (Hay House, 2013).

Neill, Michael. *The Inside-Out Revolution: The Only Thing You Need to Know to Change Your Life Forever* (Hay House, 2013).

Rackham, Neil. *SPIN Selling* (Gower, 1995).

Rubenstein, Terry, with Brian Rubenstein. *The Exquisite Mind: How a New Paradigm Transformed My Life … and Is Sweeping the World* (MX Publishing, 2016).

Sharland, Alan. *How to Resolve Bullying in the Workplace: Stepping Out of the Circle of Blame to Create an Effective Outcome for All* (CreateSpace, 2016).

Smart, Jamie. *Clarity: Clear Mind, Better Performance, Bigger Results* (Capstone, 2013).

Smith, Steven. *Catalyst: How Confidence Reacts with Our Strengths to Shape What We Achieve and Who We Become* (Veracity Press, 2014).

Index

A
agreement 29, 107, 109–111,
        123–8, 181–2
    'in principle' 29, 30
    final 94, 111, 179
    question 109–12, 114, 118,
        191
    written 126

B
Bandler, Richard 60
bargaining 98, 100, 104,
        107–116, 139, 180–81
Bottom Line 48–9, 53, 54–5,
        59, 62, 64–5, 118
brainstorming 42–3
Burns, Chantal 92
buying negotiation 24–7

C
case study
    customer-focused deals
        43–4
    flexible packages 44–5
    getting what you need 51
    Kathleen's story 19–21,
        53–4, 67–8, 92–3, 104,
        120, 128
    Simon's story 36–7, 54–5,
        93–5, 104–5, 121, 128
    Veginots 90–1
    walking away 119–20

checklist
    agreement 129
    avoiding gambits 194
    bargaining 121–2
    before you negotiate 21–2
    discussion phase 95
    mental preparation 38
    negotiating at home 183
    preparation 55
    preparing from your
        partner's point of view
        68
    proposals 105
    understanding the operating
        system 143–4
    using personality traits in
        negotiation 167
Cialdini, Robert 80
closed questions 85–7, 89
collaborative attitude 31, 39,
        57, 91–2, 177
collaborative negotiation 23,
        34–5, 51, 64, 70–71, 76,
        114, 123, 195–6
competitive negotiator 98, 162,
        185–6
conflict resolution, international
        70
constants 39–40, 46
contract, formal 103–4
Covey, Stephen 8, 57, 59,
        132

D

deadlines 115–6
Desson, Stewart 148–50, 165
discussion 69–95, 100, 102, 117, 118, 119

E

emotions 133–5, 138–40
expectations, exceeding 66–7

F

Fisher, Roger 16, 40
Fraley, R. Chris, 166
Fromm, Erich 87

G

gambits 185–94
   best of a bad choice 192
   Columbo, The 112–14, 187
   countering 193
   flinch 188
   Good Cop/Bad Cop 192–3
   higher authority 189–90
   red herring 188–9
   reluctant buyer/seller 190–1
Gottman, John 35
Grant, Adam 114–5
Green Zone of Agreement 58, 62–6, 67, 99, 118–19, 197
Grinder, John 60

H

haggling 17–19, 33
Harvard Negotiation Research Project 16
hostage negotiation 14–15, 58

Hudson, Nathan 166
human operating system 131–44

I

identifying with the other party exercise 61–2
if, the power of 72–3, 99, 108, 180–1
'If you ..., then I ...' 5, 107–8, 111, 181

J

job negotiation 19–21, 53–4, 67, 92–3, 104, 120
Journal of Economic Psychology 16

K

Kahneman, Daniel 63
Kennedy, Gavin 12

L

listening 74–9, 80, 82, 87–9, 92, 110–11, 142, 174, 178–9, 197
   Co-Active 76, 78–9, 178
   three-second pause 74, 87–9, 110–11

M

Maslow, Abraham 102
mindfulness 141–3

N

Nadella, Satya 84
Neale, Margaret 197

negotiating
    advertising sales 116–17
    at home 169–83
    bedtime 173–5, 180–81
    basic rule of 4–6
    hostage situation 14–15, 58
    job 19–21, 53–4, 67, 92–3,
        104, 120
    losing out 1–2
    salary 51, 92–3
    sales 28–30, 42, 43–4
    structure 11–13, 196, 198
    with a child 2–5, 76–8,
        171–5, 177, 179–82
negotiation exercise 90–1,
    124–5
Negotiation Journal 16
negotiation type 146–67
Negotiator, Four Types of
    Amiable 146, 158–60, 164
    Analytical 146, 156–8, 164
    Driving 146, 161–3, 164
    Expressive 146, 160–61,
        164
Neill, Michael 135
neurolinguistic programming
    60–61
non-negotiables 173

O
open questions 79–81, 82, 89

P
Patton, Bruce 16
peace negotiation 127
Personality Archetypes, Four
    147–9, 155–67

    Commanding Red 161–3
    Conscientious Blue 156–8
    Empowering Green 158–60
    Inspiring Yellow 160–61
Personality Aspects, Eight
        149–54, 163–5
    Big Picture Thinking
        150–51, 160
    Down-to-Earth 151, 156
    Extraverted 151–2, 160, 161
    Introverted 152, 156, 158
    People-Focused 152–3, 158
    Outcome-Focused 153, 161
    Discipline-Driven 153–4,
        156, 162
    Inspiration-Driven 154,
        158, 160
perspective, seeing other
        person's 57–62, 65
pitching for business 36–7,
        54–5, 93–5, 104–5, 121
preparation 12–13, 16, 19–21, 23,
        34, 39–43, 45, 49, 57, 118,
        140, 170–71, 175, 196
Proctor, Sandra 31, 145–7
proposal 97–105, 110–11, 177,
        179
psychometrics 147–9

Q
questions to ask before
        negotiating (Four P's)
        31–3, 36–7

R
Rackham, Neil 89
rapport 89–90, 136

Red Line 50–53, 59, 62, 65–6, 67–8, 81, 118, 173

S

salary negotiation 51, 53, 67–8, 92–3
sales negotiation 18–19, 24–8, 28–30, 33–4, 43–4, 112–13, 116
seven-step process 12–13, 169, 170, 196, 198
Sharland, Alan 76
'Shopping List' of variables 24, 45–6, 47, 50
Smith, Steven 9, 35
Socratic questioning 82–5

T

timeframe 11, 37, 103, 157
time-out 116–17, 139, 142
trust 15–16, 27
try it now
    asking open questions 81
    Co-Active Listening 78–9
    conversations at home 84–5
    conversations at work 85
    countering gambits 193
    creating an agreement question 110
    creating a Shopping List 46
    creating your WIN Matrices 49–50
    finding the Green Zone of Agreement 64
    finding your Eight Aspects of Personality 154
    finding your Four Colour Archetypes 163–4
    finding your partner's Four Colour Archetypes 165
    going above and beyond 66–7
    identifying with your partner 61–2
    listening 74
    observing your responses 138
    securing commitment to negotiate 30
    stating your intention to collaborate 71
    taking a time-out 117
    test your walk-away point 51
    testing variables 73
    three-second silence 88–9
    using the Four P's 33
Tulley, John 3

U

Ury, William 16

V

value, adding 40–43, 45–7
variables 39–43, 44–6, 48–9, 59, 62, 72–3, 84, 98, 111, 117, 124, 176, 180, 197

W

walking away 51–3, 119–120
WIN Matrix 47–50, 53, 54, 62, 64, 118
win-win 15–17, 23, 26–7, 31, 34, 39, 41, 113

INSPIRE TRAINING

Inspire designs bespoke development programmes that drive organizations forward, evolve and engage their workforces, and improve business performance – all leading to direct benefits to the bottom line.

Inspire is driven by its founders – Steven Fine and Gavin Presman. Steven and Gavin have a wealth of experience in developing and recruiting top performers in leading organizations in the UK and internationally.

They have extensive training and development experience, as well as a track record of building successful enterprises, and are supported by an outstanding team of associates who deliver training programmes around the world.

Inspire provides stellar business guidance across a range of areas, bringing the benefits of years of experience and innovative training tools to individuals and teams.

To discover more, or to contact Gavin directly, visit: **www.inspire-ing.co.uk**

∽

DOOR INTERNATIONAL

DOOR Training and Consulting is a global training and coaching provider, operating in over 55 countries; it is dedicated to, and passionate about, improving the performance and effectiveness of leaders, teams and organizations.

The key to DOOR's success is global expertise delivered through local know-how. DOOR translates company strategies into results, and strives to be a true solution provider for customers by understanding their needs, business strategy and structures. Together with a global strategic network, DOOR offers over 100 training and development programmes, designed to meet the latest standards and current needs of clients.

Today, the company has grown from providing training, coaching, consulting, e-learning and assessments in over 90 countries to owning the exclusive global rights to industry-leading, award-winning content that focuses on organizational culture change by means of accountability, communication and execution.

DOOR can deliver programmes based on this book in any language, across the globe.

For more information, visit: **www.doortraining.com**

⇜

INSPIRING INSIGHT

Inspiring Insight is a collection of business coaches and trainers who work with companies to improve performance, through sharing the Three Principles of Sydney Banks. Studies conducted by Inspiring Insight show the effectiveness of this approach, which centres on improving employees' resilience and state of mind, and uses companies' own Key Performance Indicators as a measure of increased effectiveness.

For more information, visit: **www.inspiringinsight.net**